Frederick Apartment

Wing: Giesecke and Dunham Residence

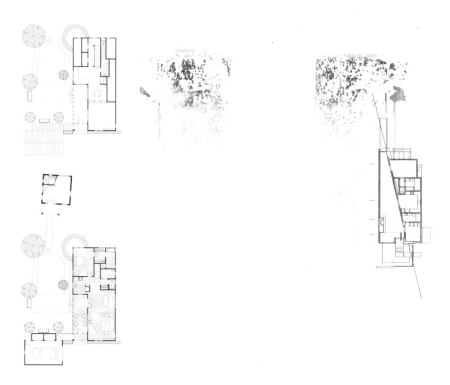

Rogers House

Collins House and Gallery

The New American Dream

First published in the United States of America in 2004
by The Monacelli Press, Inc.
902 Broadway
New York, NY 10010

Illustration Credits
Photographs on the following pages are courtesy of *Metropolitan Home* magazine: front cover, 33, 36, 38, 40, 41, 42, 43, 47, 49, 50, 51, 52, 53

Jon Miller, Hedrich Blessing: 22
Courtesy of Martha's Vineyard Historical Society: 18
Courtesy of Rob Schweitzer and the Arts & Crafts Society: 19

Front cover: Gauer Goldsmith Apartment, New York, New York
Back cover: Harrison House, Nashville, Tennessee

Library of Congress Cataloging-in-Publication Data
Gauer, James.
The new American dream : living well in small homes /
by James Gauer ;
photographs by Catherine Tighe.
    p. cm.
ISBN 1-58093-147-2
1. Small houses—United States. 2. Apartments—United States. 3. Space
(Architecture)—United States. 4. Room layout (Dwellings)—United States.
I. Tighe, Catherine. II. Title.
NA7205.G379 2004
728'.37'0973—dc22

Printed and bound in Italy
Designed by Field Study

The New American Dream

Living Well in Small Homes

By James Gauer

Photographs by Catherine Tighe

THE MONACELLI PRESS

Introduction   7

One
Modesty and the Lack of It   9
in American Housing

Two
Architectural Precedents   15
for Modest Dwellings

Three
Architectural Principles   23
and Examples

Four
How Big Small Can Be: 229
The Case for Small Dwellings

Afterword   233
Select Bibliography   237
Acknowledgments   239
Authors' Biographies   240

The New American Dream

Living Well in Small Homes

By James Gauer

Photographs by Catherine Tighe

THE MONACELLI PRESS

Introduction   **7**

One

Modesty and the Lack of It   **9**
in American Housing

Two

Architectural Precedents   **15**
for Modest Dwellings

Three

Architectural Principles   **23**
and Examples

Four

How Big Small Can Be: **229**
The Case for Small Dwellings

Afterword   **233**

Select Bibliography   **237**

Acknowledgments   **239**

Authors' Biographies   **240**

27   **Proportion**
31   Gauer Goldsmith House
45   Gauer Goldsmith Apartment

55   **Modularity**
59   Frederick Apartment
65   Wing: Giesecke Dunham Residence

79   **Scale**
83   Schultz House

93   **Transparency and Spatial Layering**
97   Brandt Ginder House

107   **Hierarchy and Procession**
111   Rogers House
125   Collins House and Gallery

135   **Light**
139   Coburn Ceccarelli Apartment
149   745 Navy Street

159   **Multifunctionalism**
163   Harrison House

175   **Simplicity**
179   Finney House

191   **Economy**
195   Bartholomew House

205   **Modesty**
209   Rice Welch House
219   Rice Welch Apartment

Introduction

I am an architect in New York City, where space is at a premium. My work includes houses and apartments of modest size, and I am passionate about the design of these small dwellings. This passion extends to my own homes. I live, by choice, in an apartment of less than five hundred square feet and in a weekend house of less than two thousand square feet. I aspire to nothing larger. I find homes of this scale to be more convenient, less expensive, and less wasteful of scarce resources. I also find them to be more architecturally expressive, more elegant, more comfortable, and ultimately more human.

My passion for small dwellings goes way back. I grew up in the suburbs of Chicago, in a simple ranch house of less than two thousand square feet. This was a normative size for suburban houses in the 1950s and '60s. When I was about twelve, I was riveted by something in one of my mother's shelter magazines. Was it a larger house that I envied? Far from it. The object of my fascination was a tiny but elegantly engineered studio apartment containing little more than a built-in daybed and two iconic Wassily chairs by Marcel Breuer. Our suburban house, modest though it may have been, was certainly more spacious and comfortable, but this one room had something—refinement? modernity?—that made spaciousness and comfort seem quite beside the point. It made anything more than one perfect room seem dowdy and unnecessary. With all the zealotry of a new convert, I was keen to transform my bedroom into a self-sufficient studio apartment, but my brother, who shared the room, did not share my enthusiasm. And so my first foray into the architecture of small spaces was thwarted. But the passion had been ignited, and nothing in the following decades has extinguished it.

This book critiques prevailing values in the realm of building and architecture, and then proposes alternatives. The small dwellings featured here represent a range of housing types, executed in a range of architectural styles. The ideal of a freestanding house with a yard is often cited as a primary cause of suburban sprawl. Yet it remains a staple of the American dream and a norm for much of the country. Therefore, many of the dwellings in this book are detached single-family homes. However, the principles that define good small dwellings apply equally to other, more urban, housing types, such as lofts and apartments.

And so I have also included a number of these. Some of these dwellings are full-time residences, while others are weekend and vacation homes. These differences are inconsequential. What all these dwellings have in common is a conviction that small is better.

These residences are illustrated not only with photographs but also with plans. Many books on architecture, especially those written for lay readers, omit these fundamental drawings. This is a mistake because plans are essential to understanding the underlying organization of any architectural design. They are the most basic component of good architecture. This is especially true of small dwellings, where every square foot has to count.

"The plan is the generator," wrote the seminal Swiss modernist architect Le Corbusier. His second great dictum, "The house is a machine for living," might mislead you into thinking that the first has something to do with electrical power. It does not. It means, quite simply, that the basic layout, or "footprint," of a dwelling determines what its overall form should be. The two-dimensional floor plan will become three-dimensional spaces. So if you don't have a good plan, you won't have good spaces.

This book is intended for lay readers. Although it may be of interest to architects, it tries to eschew the impenetrable architectural jargon that makes so many architecture books uninteresting to lay readers. Most of the architectural books offered to lay readers today are coffee table books, superficially stylish but devoid of content, and how-to books, focused narrowly on problem solving. Bookstore shelves are currently sagging under the weight of coffee table books and how-to books on small houses and apartments. There is no need for another. This book is meant as an alternative for readers who want to know more about small-scale domestic architecture, not just in the context of style and problem solving, but also in the broader context of history and ideas. And so I have tried to structure this book in favor of the latter. In doing so, I hope that I have succeeded in keeping it free of dense architectural argot and equally free of coffee table clichés. I also hope that I have succeeded in conveying my own excitement about the big architectural potential of small dwellings.

One
Modesty and the Lack of It in American Housing

The expression "Less is more" is attributed to architect Ludwig Mies van der Rohe, a pioneering modernist whose taut, crisp, and restrained designs pointed the way to an architecture of great refinement and simplicity. His corollary dictum, "God is in the details," suggested that quality was more important than quantity. But architecture was restless, fashion was fickle, and an increasingly affluent society wanted more, not less. Unparalleled economic booms in the second half of the twentieth century resulted in an explosion of housing cost, size, and architectural befuddlement. Just as the simple perfection of the Italian Renaissance had given way to the excess of the Baroque, so the simple perfection of Miesian modernism gave way to the bloated excess of postmodernism. The simple and ascetic spirit of "Less is more" gave way to the acquisitive and ironic spirit of one wag's inversion, "Less is a bore."

This book is not intended as a posthumous paean to Mies van der Rohe or to any other architect or architectural style. But the notion of less as more deserves our attention now more than ever. We live in

an age of astonishing excess, when having and wanting
more is a cultural mandate. We use our brains and
energy to work hard, and a big house or apartment
is often the visible reward for our efforts. But a smaller
house or apartment might be a much better reward,
because it takes even more brains and energy—
and, for that matter, taste—to live simply and modestly.
The cost can be measurably less, and the rewards can
be immeasurably more.

And yet simplicity and modesty elude us. Our
lives tend to be complex and chaotic and difficult to
manage. Rather than being a serene refuge from
all this complexity and chaos, our homes are often an
extension of it. And so they, too, are difficult to manage.
This difficulty stems, at least in part, from their size:
they are frequently too large. The median size of a newly
constructed single-family home in the United States
has been increasing at an alarming rate. Between
1982 and 2002, according to the U.S. Census Bureau,
it increased from 1,520 square feet to 2,114 square feet.
That's an increase of 39 percent. It seems that, even
though we are more likely to be happy with modesty
and simplicity, we tend to choose bigger houses that
burden us with excess and complexity.

One factor driving the growth of our homes is
the means by which we pay for them. The mortgage
interest tax deduction, recently coupled with low interest
rates, encourages us to justify the cost of larger homes
as safe investments to be paid for with minimum cash
and maximum mortgage. But even in after-tax dollars,
the payments can run to 30 or 40 percent of income.
The old rule of thumb was that housing should consume
no more than 25 percent of income. Today, rather than
taking advantage of low interest rates to further reduce
the cost of a smaller house, we use it to trade up to
a larger house. The higher cost of this larger house
consists of higher mortgage payments, along with higher
taxes, maintenance, and insurance. It also consists of
higher opportunity cost. When you're maxed out on
housing payments, you have little or no money left for
other investments, including retirement accounts.
The net result is a generation of homeowners struggling
to pay for large homes they can't really afford and
unable to save for retirement.

The regulations of mortgage lenders also play a
part in the bloating of America's houses. In some affluent
areas, lenders require a fixed ratio between the cost
of the land and the cost of the house. If the land is
expensive, then the house must be expensive, too. This is
true in Seaside, the little resort community on the Florida
panhandle, acclaimed for its groundbreaking urban

design. When the first generation of houses went up, they tended to be modest bungalows as small as five hundred square feet on lots that sold for under $25,000. Today, lots of similar size are selling for over $500,000. Mortgage lenders are requiring houses of equivalent cost, and so the size of new houses is pushing up over four thousand square feet.

Another reason our homes are getting bigger is that we have too many possessions. Our houses and apartments have become bloated containers for consumer goods that are too big and too numerous: overscaled furniture, oversized kitchen appliances, multiple big-screen TVs, athletic equipment for every sport and season, more toys than any child could use or want, and enough clothing to overflow all those coveted walk-in closets. We want our homes big enough to contain the trappings of affluence. And yet these rarely provide the foundation for a gracious life.

Home is as much symbol as shelter. American culture encourages hard work and rewards it with material riches. These riches are the outward signs that validate the scope and success of our ambitions. Big houses and big apartments are symbols of big aspirations and big achievements. And yet the good life they symbolize isn't necessarily what they deliver. They often lack the human scale, refinement, and architectural distinction that could facilitate, if not a good life, at least a comfortable and well-ordered life.

Excesses in our housing reflect excesses in our culture. As the sordid dramas of Enron, Tyco, WorldCom, ImClone, the New York Stock Exchange, and other corrupt corporations and agencies play themselves out, one of the recurring leitmotifs is the preposterous scale of the multiple homes of the principal players. As public revulsion at such excess grows and the fortunes of less exalted employees and unwitting shareholders dwindle, we need to rethink our attitudes toward many symptoms and symbols of excess, including housing.

There is nothing wrong with using domestic architecture as a vehicle for personal ambition. The Renaissance palazzo, the Newport cottage, and the Fifth Avenue apartment house all affirmed the wealth and position of their builders and occupants. But they also provided an elegant setting for private lives, and they made a significant contribution to public life by enriching the history of architecture and adorning the streets of our cities and towns. Today's houses and multiple dwellings typically lack architectural distinction and so are unlikely to encourage gracious living in private or cultural enrichment in public.

13

The value of houses and apartments today is determined primarily by location and size. Architectural quality counts for little, and so we see little of it. Most of the construction budget goes into maximizing square footage and supplying status-symbol appliances, finishes, fixtures, and fittings. There is very little left over for architecture. The qualities of scale and proportion that mark good architecture are too intangible to be marketed as consumer goods. And so little attention is paid to them. You'll see thousands of real-estate ads hawking granite counters and SubZero refrigerators before you see one touting a perfectly proportioned spatial sequence. On the rare occasion when architectural quality does figure into the equation, it's usually at the super luxury end of the market, where it serves as an indicator of glamour and status.

The most basic component of good architecture is a good floor plan. Good traditional plans for houses and apartments provided an elegant series of discrete rooms. Good modern plans provided free-flowing open spaces. Today's typical floor plans, for both houses and apartments, usually provide neither. Their layouts tend to be functional but banal at best, with badly proportioned, oddly shaped rooms and inelegant circulation between them. These are unlikely settings for gracious lives.

We need never pine for larger quarters if we remember this: home is not a self-contained world but a toehold in a larger world. We don't just live in our houses and apartments. We live in houses and apartments on streets in neighborhoods in communities in towns and in cities. The porch, the front stoop, the sidewalk, the street, the square, and the park expand the confines of home beyond the enclosed space of the house or apartment and into the space of the public realm. The private home is just the smallest in a series of concentric units. Seen in this context, how large does it need to be?

In the private realm, most human needs can be met at the scale of the cottage rather than at the scale of the mansion. Many new houses, lofts, and apartments, especially at the upper end of the market, have too much space. Kitchens exceed the needs of anyone but a professional cook. Great rooms lack the domestic scale essential to comfort. Master bedroom suites are so big that owners rarely leave them except to go to the kitchen. And how big does a so-called spa bathroom really need to be? Wouldn't it be cheaper, and a lot more fun, to have a smaller bathroom and go to a real spa occasionally? None of this excess is essential to living well. In fact, the elephantine inelegance of it all generally precludes living well. We can have excess or we can have the straight-forward ease and authenticity that make a gracious home. We cannot have both.

Two
Architectural Precedents for Modest Dwellings

Our houses are such unwieldy property that we are often imprisoned rather than housed in them.

The ideal of well-designed small-scale housing has a venerable tradition, and a number of distinguished architects have pursued it. The historical precedents for small dwellings are as varied as they are numerous.

Despite its reputation for ostentation and luxury, eighteenth-century France was capable of great restraint in the design of domestic interiors. At the Metropolitan Museum of Art in New York are two rooms from apartments of that time. One is a small, circular salon, the other an even smaller octagonal boudoir. Both are admirable examples of richness and elegance in tight confines. Their secret lies in their impeccable architectural proportions and details and in the corresponding scale of their furnishings.

The Palladian and neoclassical revivals in eighteenth-century England produced country houses of palatial grandeur. But they also produced exemplary small outbuildings, including workmen's cottages, whose rigorous proportions and simple classical details elevated them above their station. These small cottages were imbued with the same symmetry and harmony as their larger counterparts, but on a smaller scale. Their size was no impediment to beauty and dignity.

Much of the housing built in America in the nineteenth century came from house pattern books. Among the best of these books were two by Andrew Jackson Downing, in which he presented small but romantic cottages in a variety of styles. Downing's genius was that he used simple and natural forms appropriate for the scale of his small houses.

America's lush venerable suburbs such as Lake Forest, Illinois, and Llewellyn Park, New Jersey, are among our most beautiful landscapes. We tend to associate them with large houses and great wealth. But architectural historian Ellen Weiss believes that the ideal of single-family houses grouped together in a planned arcadia has surprisingly humble roots in the Methodist camp meetings of the mid-nineteenth century. These began as tent encampments, which were eventually replaced by miniature cities of tiny cottages of extraordinary charm. The best known of these is the village of Oak Bluffs on Martha's Vineyard.

In Victorian England, the writings of John Ruskin on art and architecture provided the philosophical basis for the Arts and Crafts movement. Ruskin's writings are notable not only for his aesthetic admonitions, but also for his moral belief that industrial capitalism owed a debt to its humblest wage earners in the form of good housing. The seeds of Ruskin's moralizing fell on fertile ground in America. The 1860s and 1870s saw the creation of small row houses, duplexes, and single-family homes in the New England mill towns of Hopedale, Massachusetts; Willimantic, Connecticut; and Ludlow, Massachusetts. The designs were good if not inventive, and the quality of the construction was high. Just south of Chicago, the Pullman Company built an entire city for its workers. This most infamous of company towns was plagued by political, social, and economic problems, but no one disputed the charm of its small brick row houses.

The need for good small dwellings was especially acute in America's cities, where decent housing for workers was in desperately short supply. In 1869 New York architect John Kellum designed Stewart's Home for Working Women on Fourth (Park) Avenue between Thirty-second and Thirty-third Streets. These small apartments provided genteel yet economical homes for department store employees and other single women. The planning was not inventive and relied too much on long corridors, but it gave birth to the residential hotel, a building type dedicated to small but respectable apartments.

Andrew Jackson Downing, A Cottage in the English or Rural Gothic Style, from *Cottage Residences*, 1842.

18

Shute (possibly), Corner of Ocean Avenue and Sea View Avenue, Oak Bluffs, Martha's Vineyard, c. 1880.

New York philanthropist Alfred Tredway White, long concerned about the abysmal housing of the immigrant poor, built model tenements in Brooklyn in the 1880s. The largest of these were the Riverside buildings, built in 1889, which were grouped around a large, landscaped courtyard and featured cross ventilation and terraces for every unit. The Progressive movement continued White's work and spawned an interest in the design of other model tenements in New York. The best of these were the Cherokee Apartments on East Seventy-eighth and Seventy-seventh Streets, overlooking the East River. Designed in 1909 by architect Henry Atterbury Smith, these handsome buildings featured vaulted entry passages with Guastavino tile and charming courtyards. Some of the apartments were as small as three hundred square feet, but each had an elegant balcony and floor-to-ceiling windows.

The continued influence of the Arts and Crafts movement is evident in many examples of good small dwellings in the late nineteenth and early twentieth centuries. The basic Arts and Crafts vocabulary of picturesque vernacular forms and humble materials in their natural state worked equally well for houses large and small. English architect C. F. A. Voysey devoted most of his career to the design of very large houses for an enlightened but decidedly wealthy Edwardian plutocracy. One of his most successful creations, however, is a humble cottage for a craftsman of modest means. Its diminutive size in no way diminishes its aesthetic power.

Another example is the work of American Arts and Crafts furniture designer and philosopher Gustav Stickley. He designed many prototypical small houses, which he presented in his magazine *The Craftsman* from 1900 through 1916. Stickley brought a true believer's zeal to the campaign for small, affordable cottages and bungalows. Some were as small as one thousand square feet, but the careful use of proportion, scale, and line always made them seem larger and more commodious.

Even as the influence of the Arts and Crafts movement waned in the early twentieth century, the development of well-designed small houses continued. From 1908 to 1940, Sears, Roebuck and Co. designed, manufactured, and sold by catalog about four hundred different models of small houses. Economical design and prefabrication made these houses affordable. Today, in neighborhoods where other houses of comparable size and age are sold as teardowns, the Sears houses command a premium and are lovingly restored.

The end of World War I saw the beginning of a housing boom for a rapidly growing middle class. The Architects' Small House Service Bureau was a nonprofit organization operated by the American Institute of Architects and endorsed by the U.S. Department of Commerce. It was formed in the early 1920s to help prospective first-time homebuilders who could not afford an architect. It provided dozens of ingenious designs, in a wide range of styles, for houses as small as three rooms. The designs were conservative miniaturizations and pastiches of larger historical prototypes. They were just the sort of architecture that modernists were prone to sneer at. But it would be a mistake to dismiss them. What these houses lacked in stylistic originality, they made up for in compact, skillful, and economical planning. They had cross ventilation. They had rooms with two and sometimes three exposures. The best of them had a clear separation of public space and private space, with modest but ample foyers and gracious living rooms. In short, they had everything you might want or need, even in a larger house.

New York City was booming in the 1920s, and the need for good small, affordable apartments was becoming a concern not only of tenement-dwelling blue-collar workers but also the rapidly growing numbers of white-collar workers. In 1928 real-estate developer Fred French began construction of Tudor City, a five-acre enclave of elegant Tudor-style buildings arranged around two parks. The complex was intended primarily for young single people working in midtown offices and contained mostly studios and one-bedrooms. The gracious architectural character of these buildings gave great dignity to the modest dwellings within. Mr. French, in marketing the apartments, coined the expression "walk to work." These apartments were conceived not as self-contained homes but as toeholds in Metropolis.

With the downsizing during the Depression, the market for large apartments in New York virtually evaporated. Prominent apartment-house architects like Emery Roth and Irwin S. Chanin adapted their sophisticated planning strategies for larger apartments to the design of smaller ones. As a result, apartments that might have been mean and tight became elegant and gracious. The best of these apartments had generous foyers, which provided not only efficient circulation but also a sense of spaciousness far in excess of the actual square footage.

Good small dwellings were a high priority for the first generation of modern architects. Le Corbusier, for example, was deeply committed to the democratic ideal of well-designed housing for the working class. The architectural quality of his working-class houses and apartments far surpasses that of typical middle- and upper-class dwellings today. The designs of Le Corbusier

Sears, Roebuck and Co., Modern Home No. 126, Modern Homes Catalog, 1909.

Frank Lloyd Wright, Kentuck Knob, Chalk Hill, Pennsylvania, 1953.

are especially noteworthy for their innovative open plans and generous windows, made economically feasible by mass production. Another early modernist who tackled the small house with artistic aplomb was the Viennese Adolf Loos, whose great gift was an ability to organize the spaces within a small house as complex geometric puzzles.

In 1929 Frank Lloyd Wright designed a small apartment tower, intended for a New York site. Each floor contained four duplexes with high studio living rooms and balconies. Their compact elegance was made possible by their ingenious polygonal planning. Unfortunately, the project was never built in New York, but a variation of it was constructed as an office tower in Oklahoma. It has recently been renovated as a stylish luxury hotel.

From 1929 to 1943, Wright, in the third phase of his prolific career, designed over fifty small, moderately priced houses, in sizes starting at 870 square feet. These were his Usonian houses, and they set the bar for architectural ambition in small houses as high as it has ever been. These houses typically had an open plan in which entry, living, dining, kitchen, and working spaces flowed together around a central fireplace and service core. Generous use of casement windows and French doors blurred the line between indoors and out, thus expanding the perceived space.

From 1945 until 1962, the Los Angeles–based magazine *Arts & Architecture*, edited by John Entenza, commissioned the design of thirty-six houses, known as the Case Study Houses. Twenty-three of these were built in southern California, in sizes as small as 1,100 square feet. Among the architects participating in this program were Pierre Koenig, Craig Ellwood, Richard Neutra, Charles Eames, and Eero Saarinen. Entenza wanted the post–World War II housing boom to be the occasion for serious architecture. So he began this program in which his magazine would be the client for new houses of small size but large design ambition. The program was hugely successful. It produced an iconic body of work that combined new materials and economical building techniques with a disciplined modern sensibility. Of the twenty-three houses completed, twelve were awarded prizes by the American Institute of Architects.

The Farnsworth House by Mies van der Rohe, an iconic and elegant steel-and-glass pavilion overlooking the Fox River in Plano, Illinois, was designed to have only one bedroom. It is generally regarded as one of the most beautiful of all twentieth-century houses, not in spite of its size but because of it. The secret of its success is twofold. First is its open plan: spaces are delineated only by wall planes that appear to float, cabinetry that stops short of the ceiling, and furniture groupings. This allows space to flow freely within the interior volume. Second is the separation of exterior walls into thin structural columns and continuous planes of glass. This erases all visual distinction between interior space and exterior space. The history of this house epitomized the conflict between a client in search of comfort and an architect in search of perfection. Cost overruns, a romantic entanglement, and a lawsuit all conspired to heighten the drama.

Mies also designed several elegant and inventive apartment houses, most of them in Chicago. The first of these was the seminal 860 Lake Shore Drive. It has always been considered a luxe address, but in fact, many of its apartments are studios. The planning of these apartments is similar to that of the Farnsworth House. Spaces are defined by groupings of furniture and cabinets and by walls so few and so abstract they appear to be floating planes. The floor-to-ceiling windows provide expansive views of Lake Michigan and dematerialize the rooms' perimeter.

Any of these examples alone, but certainly all of them together, might have established a tradition of dignified small dwellings strong enough to withstand the late-twentieth-century onslaught of McMansions and cheesy "luxury" apartments. We would do well to ask where they might have led us, had we paid more attention to them. And we might hope that they will yet inspire future generations of architects, developers, and owners to carry on in a similar spirit.

The architects whose work is featured in this book have paid attention to historical precedents. Martha Finney's charming farmhouse evokes the simple cottages of Andrew Jackson Downing. The Rogers House by Ryall Porter Architects is modeled on the traditional side-porch-entry houses of Charleston, South Carolina. The Giesecke and Dunham House pays homage to the Usonian houses of Frank Lloyd Wright. The architectural language of 745 Navy Street owes a clear debt to the Case Study Houses. The Brandt Ginder House recalls the compact villas of Adolf Loos. Robert Schultz's house for his parents both works within and transforms the local beach-cottage vernacular of its waterfront community. Price Harrison's house harkens back to the exquisite minimalism of the Farnsworth House. Emery Roth's inventive apartment planning influenced my own tiny apartment. And my weekend house was influenced by historical sources ranging from vernacular sheds to Italian villas.

Mies van der Rohe, Farnsworth House, Plano, Illinois. 1946–50.

22

Three
Architectural Principles and Examples

Beauty results from naturalness, from simplicity, and from good proportions.

The Architects' Small House Service Bureau

The design of small spaces requires no magic. It requires an understanding of basic human needs. It requires an ability to manipulate space. It requires a willingness to abandon conventional thinking. And it requires adherence to ten principles:

1. **Proportion**
2. **Modularity**
3. **Scale**
4. **Transparency and Spatial Layering**
5. **Hierarchy and Procession**
6. **Light**
7. **Multifunctionalism**
8. **Simplicity**
9. **Economy**
10. **Modesty**

These ten principles apply to dwellings of all sizes, but they apply especially to small houses and apartments. Their impact on a small space is usually more intense than on a large space. The small dwelling intensifies these principles in the same way that a small photographic print intensifies the resolution of the image. They can inform a wide variety of decisions to be made and problems to be solved in designing, building, and renovating. They can, if we pay attention to them, transform our small houses and apartments into places of great beauty, utility, and comfort.

The very notion of adhering to principles is somewhat at odds with the contemporary image of architects as willful artists, hell-bent on originality for its own sake. This is an unlikely persona for the self-effacing discipline of adhering to principles. Fortunately, the image bears little resemblance to reality. Many architects today, especially those at work on small dwellings, are indeed creative and artistic. But theirs is an art firmly grounded in principles.

All of the dwellings described on the following pages embody, to some degree, all of these principles. But each one is an especially adept illustration of one principle in particular.

Proportion

Proportion is the good breeding of architecture.
It is that something, indefinable to the unprofessional
eye, which gives repose and distinction to a room:
in its origin a matter of nice mathematical calculation,
of scientific adjustment of voids and masses, but in
its effects as intangible as that all-pervading essence
that the ancients called the soul.

Edith Wharton

The first principle is proportion. Proportion refers to mathematical relationships between the dimensions of architectural elements. The height, length, and width of a house or a room or even of smaller elements such as doors, windows, moldings, fireplaces, and furnishings should relate to each other in a harmonious way. Most important, they should relate to you. Human scale is where proportion should lead.

Basic geometric figures like squares and rectangles provide us with the fundamental tools of proportion. For example, rooms that are squares, or multiples of squares, seem restful to the human eye. Windows that are tall rectangles seem well suited to the verticality of the human body. Proportional relationships are mathematical, but you don't have to be a mathematician, or even a keen observer of rooms and windows, to know when a room is well proportioned or badly proportioned. We sense these things intuitively. That's the beauty of proportion. All the appropriately dimensioned components add up to a serene and subtly perceptible whole. A well-proportioned room imparts a satisfying sense of order and calm, and you don't even have to know why. This is especially true in a small room, where good proportions can make up for a lack of square footage.

Proportion establishes a coherent system of visual relationships in buildings and spaces of any size. It bestows aesthetic consistency on disparate functional and technical components. The resulting sense of order and continuity is especially valuable in small dwellings, where there is simply no space for parts out of synch with each other or with the whole.

Repose, distinction, and soul: What more could we ask of our homes? A well-proportioned small dwelling is infinitely more likely to have these attributes than a badly proportioned dwelling of any size.

Small in Town and Small in the Country: Two Tiny Essays in Proportion

This small Connecticut weekend house and even smaller New York City apartment, both of which I designed for my partner, Joel Goldsmith, and myself, illustrate the dogged pursuit of proportion in a complementary pair of small dwellings.

Gauer Goldsmith House
Sharon, Connecticut
1,800 square feet
Architect: Gauer + Marron Studio

This house in the Litchfield Hills of northwest Connecticut, less than an hour from Edith Wharton's house in the Berkshires, is an object lesson in proportion. The massing and organization of the house are mathematically precise. The house is essentially a cube whose top has been cut away to the shape of a gabled roof. The bottom of the cube has been partially burrowed into its hillside site. The cube has been divided on a two-foot grid, which organizes not only the house and its rooms, but also the adjacent porches, courtyard, and garage. The grid assures that all elements of the house are harmoniously proportioned.

The square plan of the house is recalled in the plans of its rooms, which are either squares or rectangles based on squares, and in the dimensions of typical elements. Window sashes, for example, are typically two by four feet, or two squares high. These are used to create both long horizontal bands in the smaller rooms and large squares in the largest room. Relationships like these are the basic components of the architectural good breeding Edith Wharton held so dear. And yet, for all its mathematical precision, this house looks little like a cube, well bred or not, and much like a vernacular shed.

The house measures less than two thousand square feet. From the road, it appears to be a cluster of small agricultural sheds with painted wood siding and metal roofs. The only clue that something more sophisticated might be happening here is that the siding, upon closer inspection, is actually a rigorous grid, which articulates the house's two-foot planning module and precisely frames the doors and windows.

In spite of its simple vernacular form, the house is organized like a miniature Italian villa, a prototype of proportional refinement. Between the garage and the porch is an entry courtyard. Though the detailing of the house is thoroughly modern, the courtyard is thoroughly classical and includes gravel walks, parterres planted in boxwood, and a fountain, albeit one made from a galvanized livestock trough.

The courtyard is laid out on the house's two-foot planning grid and organized around its major axis, which leads from the fountain to a gravel path, up a monumentally overscaled staircase to a covered porch. It then continues through the front door, into a low-ceilinged foyer, through a pair of French doors, and finally into a large two-story living and dining room, overlooked by an interior balcony. More French doors give onto an exterior balcony and a view of the Berkshires. It's the spatial sequence of a classical villa, from enclosed courtyard to open vista, with very little lost in the downsizing.

The secret of the house's success is that within its small, gabled shed lies a complex series of carefully proportioned interlocking spaces, all adhering to a strict hierarchy, in the manner of Adolf Loos. The big volumetric gesture is the two-story living and dining room. Its classical proportions make it as tall as it is wide and half again as long. Entering it through the small low-ceilinged cubic foyer heightens its dramatic effect and makes it seem even larger. All other rooms are also carefully proportioned, but on a smaller scale, in deference to the one big room.

Would Edith Wharton have approved of a house that aspires to be a villa but conceals those aspirations within an assemblage of simple sheds? We'll never know, but it's unlikely she would have found fault with its proportions.

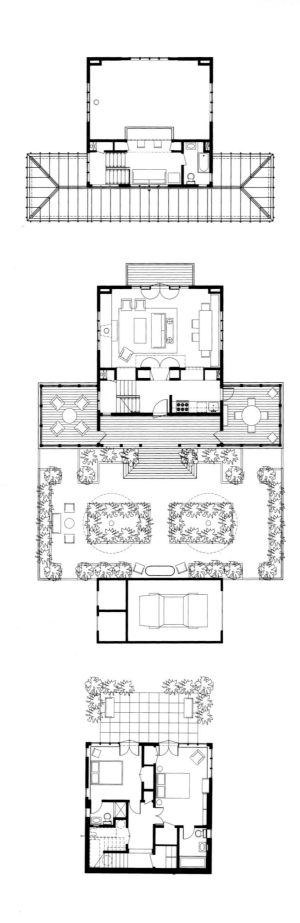

Gauer Goldsmith Apartment
New York, New York
500 square feet
Architect: Gauer + Marron Studio

This five-hundred-square-foot junior one-bedroom apartment in midtown Manhattan was originally a studio with a Murphy bed and an efficiency kitchen. Despite its tiny size, it offered several advantages. First, it had a midtown location, which made it convenient to go to the Connecticut house by train from Grand Central Terminal. Second, it had a terrace with panoramic skyline views. Third, it had exposures on two sides, a rare luxury that made it possible to add a small bedroom. Fourth and most interesting architecturally, the plan of the space had the highly desirable proportions of a double square.

Rooms that are based on geometric figures like squares can be very satisfying. The double square proportions of this apartment made its elegant layout possible. In addition to peripheral spaces containing closets, bath, and a tiny kitchen, the apartment was essentially one big rectangle, twelve feet wide by twenty-eight feet long. A big beam and two engaged columns in the center divided the space approximately into two squares. The square with the French doors to the terrace was the obvious living room. The other square had to be everything else: foyer, bedroom, storage, and space to expand the kitchen.

The new plan called for the apartment to be gutted. A ship's-cabin bedroom was placed in front of a west-facing window with a view of the Chrysler Building. In order to create the illusion of a small loft, the bedroom was treated as a miniature building floating within the larger space. No actual walls enclose it. Rather, it's surrounded by much needed cabinetry along with clerestory windows and sliding glass pocket doors. These elements suggest the exterior elevations of a small building. The apartment's original steel-and-glass casement windows are beautifully proportioned. They are also its most distinctive feature, and so the new interior doors and windows were fabricated to match. All of these elements were positioned on a rigorous system of axes and cross axes to maximize vistas through the apartment. The Chrysler Building, for example, is visible not only from the bedroom but also from the foyer thanks to an interior window that extends the axis of the bedroom's exterior window. Architectural details are minimal and uncluttered, so as not to distract the eye from the simple but refined proportions of the space.

A new stainless-steel kitchen extends beyond the confines of the previous kitchen and now contains all the amenities, including a dishwasher and ample counter space. The bathroom stayed where it was but got a full makeover in glossy white tiles and simple high-quality fixtures and fittings. The bathroom door, like all others at the perimeter of the apartment, is a frameless "concealed door" on pivot hinges. This allows the wall planes to remain unbroken, contributing to a greater sense of spaciousness. All the perimeter surfaces are painted semigloss white. All the cabinetry that encloses the bedroom is painted high-gloss white. This subtle distinction helps to distinguish the "miniature building" of the bedroom from the larger space that contains it.

Not squandering precious square footage on a large bedroom allowed for one extravagant spatial gesture: an ample and classically proportioned entry foyer much larger than might be expected in such a modest apartment. This makes the experience of entering the apartment extraordinarily gracious, with sufficient space for chair, console, mirror, and sconces— all the accoutrements of a much grander space. Thoughtful attention to proportion made all this urbane elegance possible in just five hundred square feet.

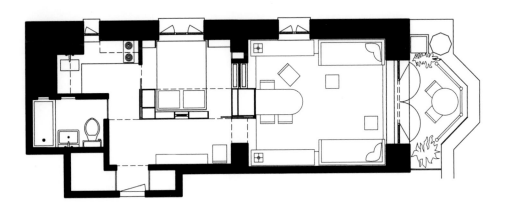

Modularity

The regulating line is a means to an end.
It is not a recipe.

Le Corbusier

Modularity is really just a variation on proportion. It is classical proportion tempered by modern industrial standardization. Modularity is the modern method of achieving proportion and economy at the same time. Le Corbusier developed a proportioning system, which he called the Modulor. He used it to order "the dimensions of that which contains and that which is contained." This system was grounded both in geometry and in the proportions of the human body. It used mathematics to achieve harmony.

Pioneering modernists like Le Corbusier were not alone in appreciating the benefits of modularity. American architect H. T. Lindeberg was a very fashionable designer of lavish country houses in a variety of period styles in the years after World War I. But the demand for large houses evaporated in the Depression, and Lindeberg turned his attention to the design of small houses built from prefabricated components. Plans, sections, and elevations were organized on a grid of two-foot and four-foot modules. Not only did the prefab modules allow great economy in construction, they also regulated the proportions of all architectural elements. In Lindeberg's modest Depression-era dwellings, mathematical precision and technological ingenuity collaborated to create elegance and human scale.

Architects have a sometimes-deserved reputation for being a bit uptight. This reputation is enhanced by their propensity to think and design in terms of grids. Free spirits may chafe at the notion of living in a house whose origins are related to graph paper, but the grid is an extraordinarily useful tool. It allows the architect to think simultaneously of well-proportioned rooms, doors, and windows and of modular—and therefore economical—ways of achieving them. Bricks and concrete blocks come in standard eight-inch modules. Stock windows are sized to coordinate with those brick sizes. And plywood comes in sheets measuring four by eight feet. The architect who bears these modules in mind can deliver to his client a nicely proportioned house built at a reasonable cost.

Modulating a Small Shelter in a Big Barn

Frederick Apartment
Bucks County, Pennsylvania
440 square feet
Designer: Jack Frederick Design

Furniture designer and maker Jack Frederick knows how to work with modules. Friends had been allowing him to use their early-nineteenth-century barn in rural Bucks County, Pennsylvania, as a studio. He dreamed of building his own house but couldn't yet afford to buy land. So Frederick's friends agreed to let him build a temporary modular apartment within the confines of their barn. One day he would acquire some land and reconfigure this modular home on a new and permanent foundation, but in the meantime, this was a rare opportunity to combine his need for shelter with his ideas about prefabricated modules.

Frederick's approach to construction called for conventional two-by-four and two-by-six wood stud framing for prefinished insulated panels roughly four feet wide and eight feet high. Each one was light enough to be moved by two people. The air spaces between the studs provided a high insulation value, which protected the space from cold in the winter and heat in the summer. They also offered protection from dampness in the woods just behind the property. These panels became the basic module of the walls and ceiling. When assembled, they became a freestanding object within the post-and-beam structure of the barn. The architectural notion of a house within a house is rather familiar. Frederick's notion of a house within a barn, on the other hand, is rather novel.

Some of the materials were salvaged, such as the stained pine flooring and the sliding glass doors that were used as mobile room dividers. Frederick bought the rest of the materials over time. The construction process took four years. During that time, he lived on the site and did the work himself.

The design evolved even as it was being built. The reality of living in a small enclosed space led to the idea of hinged ceiling panels, for example. These could be opened to the sounds and smells of the neighboring woods on warm summer nights.

The space was quite small, at 440 square feet. This mandated an open plan, in which the space was used in four parallel rectangular layers: kitchen, sleeping, office, and living. There were no barriers between these spaces other than sliding doors and drapery. There was no conventional bathroom. The kitchen sink doubled as a bathroom sink. A shower stall with a hinged partition sat next to the refrigerator. A composting toilet was located in an outhouse. And a salvaged clawfoot bathtub overlooking a secluded pasture was available for bathing in warm weather.

Frederick saw his modular enclosure as a membrane through which "the quietness of nature can filter through and encourage an uncluttered and low-maintenance life." It was deliberately temporary and no longer exists in its former state. The modules have been disassembled and put in storage, along with the clawfoot tub. Frederick looks forward to reassembling them into another miniature, but more permanent, castle.

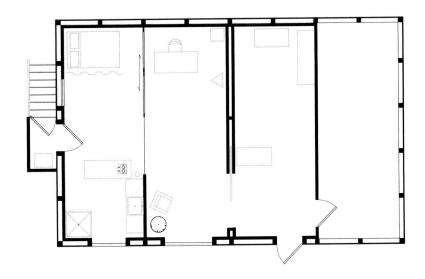

Modulating a Dialogue between Architecture and Nature

Wing: Giesecke Dunham Residence
Landenberg, Pennsylvania
1,200 square feet
Architect: MERZBAUarchitecture

Anyone who fears that a modulated design will produce a dull gridded house with all the appeal of a shrink-wrapped box should study this sculptural gem by architect Donald Dunham and rest easy. Dunham designed this 1,200-square-foot house for himself and his wife, Annette Giesecke, on four acres of steeply wooded hillside overlooking a five-thousand-acre nature preserve in southeastern Pennsylvania.

Dunham and Giesecke love the outdoors and wanted their house to reflect that. His primary goal in designing the house was to establish "a dialogue between the built and the natural." He achieved this by organizing the house along mathematical guidelines that both anchored the house to the earth and created vistas between interior and exterior. Dunham explains his strategy:

> Horizontal organization utilizes a three-foot module, the minimum passage width. The eight-inch vertical module is based on the standard concrete masonry unit. The confluence of the two

modules is expressed at the six-foot spacing of the
vertical window mullions. This allows views through
the house, framing unexpected interior and exterior
landscapes. These are not happy accidents! They
are the result of carefully studied models and rigid
geometric protocols.

This modular geometry expresses itself in a plinth of concrete-block walls, which rise up from the natural grade and thereby tether the structure to the site. But lest the house seem too grounded, Dunham added a kinetic counterpoint: a butterfly roof, or "wing" as he calls it, which gave the house its name. This roof, he says, "is an element designed to float or hover within the forest canopy when glimpsed from the preserve below, not as a permanent recognizable form, but as a transitory kinetic entity."

The two-winged roof has functions beyond the poetic. The larger wing to the south shields the house and its elevated terrace from both rain and sun. And it ties the house to its site by running parallel to the slope of the land. The smaller northern wing is pitched more steeply to provide northern light to the interior and to suggest a sense of flight. Between the plinth and the hovering roof wings, nothing more than a continuous glass membrane of windows and doors separates indoors from out.

According to Dunham, the interior of the house is also carefully modulated:

Most of the interior doors pocket into the walls,
creating different configurations of privacy, light,
and perception. This modulation of space is crucial
when designing smaller dwellings.

Dunham cites several key influences on his modular approach to the small house. Both he and Giesecke had lived in large cities and learned that efficient storage made gracious living possible in small flats. They also had the good fortune to live in two architecturally distinguished small houses. The first, by New Zealand's inventive vernacularist Ian Athfield, was notable for its site-specific and unorthodox compactness. The second was designed in 1947 by Los Angeles architect Whitney P. Smith as an experiment in prefabricated building techniques and the use of simple but versatile materials like plywood. In 1950 the house was renovated to the design of a young protégé of Frank Lloyd Wright. It emerged from this process looking remarkably like Wright's Usonian houses.

"Wing," on the other hand, no matter how many influences it may have absorbed, looks like nothing other than itself: a small dwelling of great power and originality.

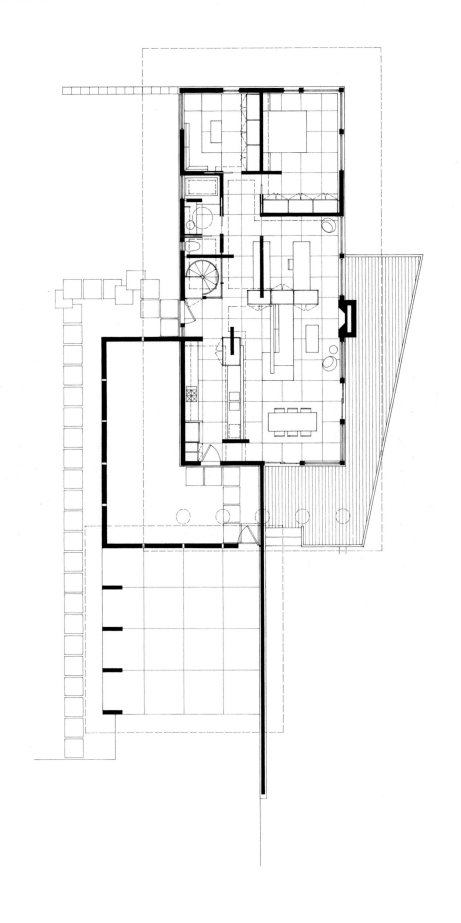

Scale

Always design a thing by considering it in its
next larger context—a chair in a room, a room
in a house, a house in an environment.

Eliel Saarinen

Scale, like modularity, is a corollary of proportion. If proportion refers to mathematical relationships between the dimensions of architectural elements, then scale refers to perceived relationships between the overall sizes of those elements. Proportion is about the height of a door relative to its width. Scale is about the overall size of that door relative to the size of an adjacent window. It is also about the size of that door relative to the size of the person who walks through it.

The relative sizes of doors, windows, ceiling heights, and other architectural components should, as a rule, be in synch with one another. They should also, as a rule, be in synch with the dimensions and proportions of the human body. The architect who knows how to do this also knows how to throw these dimensions and proportions deliberately out of synch. This puts at his disposal a powerful tool for the design of small dwellings: the manipulation of scale. A design move as simple as enlarging a single window can create multiple scales within a facade. This in turn can rescue its composition from monotony, mark the location of an important space, and enlarge our perception of the overall size of the house.

Scale is a component of all good architecture. But in a small dwelling, where the sizes of spaces and elements are likely to confound conventional perceptions of both building scale and human scale, it must be used with extraordinary skill and ingenuity. If a small house is to look like something more than a human-size wren coop, an architect with a keen eye for scale must study the size and placement of ceilings, doors, windows, stairs, trim, and all the other elements that add up to an architectural whole. The same is true of a small apartment that aspires to look like something more than a walk-in closet with windows. All the proportion and modularity in the world won't produce good small dwellings without the thoughtful treatment of scale.

Two-Faced:
Scale and Duality

Schultz House
Beach Haven, New Jersey
1,250 square feet
Architect: Robert Schultz

Architect Robert Schultz designed this 1,250-square-foot beach cottage for his parents. "Its character," says Schultz, "is inseparable from its location and history." The location is Long Beach Island, an eighteen-mile-long sandbar off the New Jersey coast. The history is that of a mass-produced beach resort of small look-alike cottages, developed after World War II as a sort of waterfront Levittown, "where sand dunes and bayberry groves were leveled and thousands of look-alike cottages were built on a grid of numbered streets." Robert Schultz's grandparents bought one of these cottages in 1963. His parents inherited it in 1990 and planned to use it as a retirement home. A severe Nor'easter destroyed it only two years later, in 1992, the same year their son graduated from architecture school.

The Schultzes clung to their dream of a waterfront retirement cottage and decided to rebuild. The size of the house was determined by constraints of budget and zoning. The budget was limited to a modest insurance settlement and some savings. The local code required the new house to maintain the precise footprint and square footage of the old house. Added to these constraints was Schultz's sensitivity to the character of the street where the house was located. The houses are all of an anonymous type that Schultz calls "the island's 1950s developer vernacular." Neither Schultz nor his parents wanted to break with this type and build an ostentatious replacement for a teardown.

But the street was not the only context from which Schultz could take his cues. There was also the water. And therein lay his opportunity. "At the back of the house," he says, "the context is quite different. In contrast to the small scale and repetitive look of the street, there is the big scale and visual variety of the harbor."

The simple idea of the front and the back was my initial approach to the house. While the front was anonymous, symmetrical and small-scale, the back was particular, asymmetrical and large-scale. The bland decorum of the front molds into the expressive individuality of the rear.

The basic elements of roof, wall, and window became Schultz's primary tools for achieving this inspired duality. On the street, these elements compose themselves deferentially, even primly, into a slightly abstracted Cape Cod cottage. On the water, they explode into its opposite. The wall and roof splay into a butterfly shape, the inverse of the Cape Cod gable. And the sizes and shapes of the windows are transformed from four equal units symmetrically placed to three unequal units of graduated size and asymmetrical placement. The real scale buster is the large square corner window, which marks the largest interior space and affords spectacular views. As Schultz explains, "It opens up the small house by introducing a large scale."

Duality of scale is a very sophisticated game. In this, his first project, Robert Schultz has played it with remarkable finesse.

84

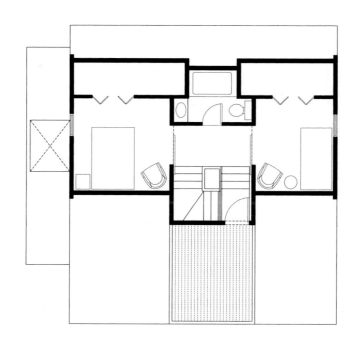

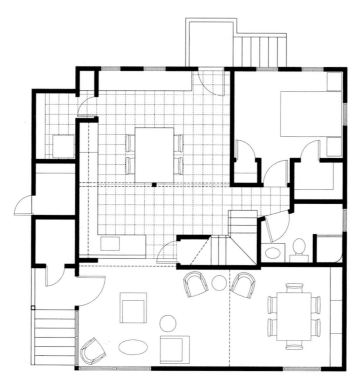

Transparency
and Spatial Layering

Illusion is the first of all pleasures.

Oscar Wilde

The way rooms interlock with each other and with the outdoors is much more important than their size. Multiple spaces that open to each other and to nature can have a sense of spaciousness much greater than the sizes of the individual spaces might suggest.

Transparency and spatial layering are important principles to follow in order to achieve the illusion of more space. Transparency does not mean having a glass house or an apartment with floor-to-ceiling windows, though these can certainly help to create transparency. Nor does it mean any of the fashionable twaddle that current architectural theorists assign to it. Transparency simply means being able to see through a house or a space, from front to back or side to side or inside to out or all three. Spatial layering is the means of achieving transparency, by creating vistas through multiple layers of spaces.

There are two great devices for creating spatial layering, one classical and the other modern. The classical device is the enfilade. This is simply a series of rooms that open to each other along a single axis. The marvel of an enfilade is that the rooms, no matter what their size, maintain their individual identities as enclosed spaces while still creating a powerful sense of openness. Two small rooms, with one big opening between them, can pack a powerful spatial punch.

The enfilade dates back to seventeenth-century France and really came to the fore domestically in the design of nineteenth-century bourgeois apartments in Paris. If you've ever wandered through the galleries of the Metropolitan Museum in New York or the National Gallery in Washington, D.C., you've experienced an enfilade. In these very large buildings, the enfilade is used to break down the vast square footage of the museum into smaller, more intimate rooms suitable for displaying paintings. But you can use it in reverse. By joining small rooms together through aligned openings, you allow each individual room to gain perceived space from the adjacent rooms.

The modern device for creating spatial layering is the open plan, which proposes the elimination of fully enclosed rooms in favor of large open spaces. Rather than connecting multiple smaller spaces to add up to a larger whole, the open plan creates a single large space and then suggests smaller spaces within it. The concept was shaped and developed by numerous early modern architects, including Frank Lloyd Wright and Mies van der Rohe. In Wright's houses, multiple spaces are anchored by central cores, usually fireplaces, around which the spaces flow. In Mies's houses and apartments, a single rectangular volume is interrupted only by cabinetry and floating wall planes, which merely suggest the enclosure of space. And the exterior walls are frequently reduced to continuous planes of glass, making the barrier between interior and exterior virtually invisible. In an open plan, full-height walls do not enclose the spaces. Instead, individual spaces are only partially enclosed or suggested by cabinetry, furniture, changes in ceiling height, flooring, and any number of other devices.

No matter how they are achieved, by means traditional or modern, transparency and spatial layering can transform not only interior space but also the relationship between interior space and exterior space. The skillful use of glass can extend the perceived space of the house out into the landscape. And the artful positioning and sizing of openings can frame vistas and modulate light.

Transparency
and Nature

Brandt Ginder House
Mechanicsburg, Pennsylvania
1,235 square feet
Architect: Brandt + Ginder Architecture, Inc.

Architects Suzanne Brandt and Barry Ginder designed for themselves a house that embodies transparency with great skill and refinement. But you wouldn't know it at first glance. The exterior of the house, with its simple brick volume, might suggest solidity or opacity rather than transparency. But that appearance is deceptive.

The architects were motivated "to design a dwelling for ourselves shaped not by style, but by desired experiences of light, wind, exterior views, and interior relationships." These experiences are the very essence of transparency.

The path to attaining their goals began with siting the house on its gently sloping two and a half acres in rural Mechanicsburg, Pennsylvania. The siting, says Ginder, promotes "natural light throughout the day and stargazing by night to activate the spaces." The house is oriented away from the road and toward the private fields and pastures to the southeast. Locating the double-height living room at the southeast corner and raising it up to the *piano nobile*, or second level, allowed the architects to reframe specific views of the landscape—

"almost as paintings on the wall," explains Brandt. "The view through the upper south wall window, from across the double-height space, collapses the distant horizon into the immediate vicinity and has been referred to as our 'Hudson River Valley landscape painting.' "

The trajectory of the sun as it moves around the house determined the size and placement of windows. Clerestories to the east bring the morning sun into the bedroom and bathroom. The arc of the sun then continues through the kitchen and dining areas and into the tall, overscaled windows of the double-height living space through midday. In the late afternoon and evening, clerestories above a catwalk maintain the light in the double-height room by bringing it in from the west.

One especially clever device that underscores the transparency of the house is the mahogany ceiling that continues from interior to exterior. Not only does this ceiling cast a warm orange glow when it captures the light, but it visually extends the limits of the interior spaces, suggesting greater volume than they actually have. This device is most effective at the two porches, one at the entry and another off the double-height space. Here, the mahogany clads not only the ceiling but also the walls, suggesting that these spaces have been carved out of the house's simple brick volume. The porches become both extensions of the house into the landscape and extensions of the landscape into the house.

Because the footprint of the house is so compact, at 690 square feet, the interior had to be flexible and open yet still provide some separation and variety of spaces. "In lieu of drywall partitions throughout the house," says Ginder, "figural compositions of cabinetry accessible from both sides were inserted to divide, shape and/or connect spaces." The result is a skillful contrast between the larger spaces and, as Brandt notes, "peripheral spaces to linger and reflect."

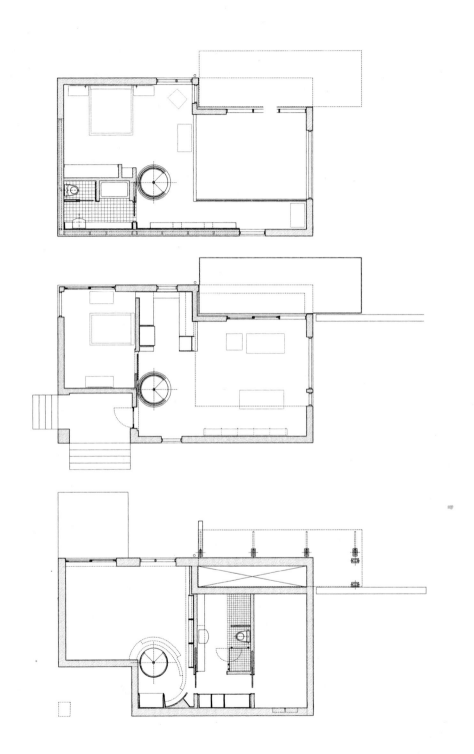

Hierarchy
and Procession

I must create a system, or be enslaved by
another man's.

William Blake

No, this section is not about religion. It's about how spaces are organized and how we move through them. In a small house or apartment, it is essential to establish a hierarchy of spaces and apportion location, square footage, and volume accordingly. The term hierarchy may seem more appropriate for a large house, where many rooms must be organized and stratified. But it's equally appropriate for a small house or apartment, where only one space can be large and all other spaces must be deferentially smaller. Such a house can be spatially surprising and very comfortable.

Hierarchy is a variation on scale. Scale is about the relative sizes of architectural elements. Hierarchy is about the relative importance of architectural spaces. The differences between spaces, whether functional or symbolic, indicate their relative importance in a dwelling's composition and therefore in its hierarchy. These differences are expressed in size, shape, and location.

In a small dwelling, the most important space is usually the living room or its open-plan equivalent, the multipurpose living area. Within the overall composition of the house, it should be located to express its primacy and to take the best advantage of light and views. This space will invariably be given the largest share of the dwelling's limited square footage. It should also be given the largest share of its volume.

Volume is a corollary of hierarchy. It is architecture's three-dimensional element, the void defined by walls, ceiling, and floor. A room with a higher ceiling has more volume than a room of the same length and width with a lower ceiling. The taller room seems larger because it is larger, even though its square footage, measured in two dimensions, is the same. In a spatial hierarchy, it's the third dimension that counts, and the space with greatest volume is usually on top.

As for procession, the journey is as important as the destination. If you have to pass through multiple layers of space to reach your destination, you'll really feel like you're going somewhere. If each of those spatial layers is part of a larger hierarchy, then both the destination and the journey will be richer experiences. The approach to the big space is especially critical. If you walk right into it from the street, you've blown the surprise. But if you enter it through a processional sequence of smaller spaces, then the importance of the big space is slowly revealed and firmly established.

Discreet
and Evocative

Rogers House
New Albany, Mississippi
1,650 square feet
Architect: Ryall Porter Architects

Ted Porter understands hierarchy and procession. He has used them skillfully in this 1,650-square-foot house for his mother, Jimmie Rogers, in New Albany, Mississippi, birthplace of William Faulkner. He did this by taking an iconically simple house form, the gabled shed, and investing it with a clear but subtle spatial hierarchy and a deliberate processional path.

The plan of the house is modeled on the side-porch-entry houses indigenous to Charleston, South Carolina. On an urban site, entry from the side offers practicality in the layout of rooms. It also offers one of the by-products of hierarchy: an indirect path with a subtle suggestion of mystery and grandeur that can make a small house seem like a big deal.

Anyone who has seen the BBC series based on E. F. Benson's *Mapp and Lucia* knows this. Miss Mapp's house (in reality Henry James's house) is the grandest in town, coveted by the socially ambitious Lucia. But the house looks very discreet and unassuming from the street. There is no clue to its internal elegance until you realize it has no conventional front door. Rather, the house has a discreet door to an entry courtyard off to the side. It's the courtyard entry that first suggests the grandeur of the house and tells you its owner is someone to be reckoned with.

The side-porch plan allowed Porter to create a similarly evocative house by establishing a hierarchical sequence of spaces. The sequence begins at the motor court, where the simple vernacular facade of the house belies a sophisticated interplay of hierarchy and scale. "The front facade is simple," explains Porter, "yet the single large window creates a tension in the way the scale of the house is perceived."

A modest door is tucked discreetly into a small, open entry porch to the side. It does not open into the house directly. Rather, it opens into the screened side porch. So begins a carefully calibrated procession from the motor court through the small entry porch and into the long, rectangular screened porch. In the first half of the screened porch, windows to the right provide a glimpse into the living room. Screened openings to the left provide a glimpse into the garden. But these openings provide no access, only evocation. There is no choice but to keep moving into the second half of the screened porch, where the ceiling jumps up and the scale explodes to reveal a multiplicity of second-floor windows and first-floor doors. Here, a clear choice presents itself: a screen door on the left leads to the garden, and a pair of French doors on the right leads indoors to the dining area, where another choice presents itself: go further back into the private zone of the house or return toward the front into the spatial surprise of the two-story living room.

The size, shape, and location of the living room all indicate that it is the terminus of the processional sequence and the climax of the spatial hierarchy. Not only is it the largest room in the house, it also has the most compelling shape and the greatest volume. Its shape is that of a cube partially shorn away by the gabled roof. This modification, rather than compromising some geometric purity, creates considerable spatial drama. The location of the room, even more than its size or shape, indicates its primacy. It sits alone at the front of the house, with three exposures, so it gets light from three directions. "Where views to neighboring houses exist," says Porter, "small punched windows are placed to allow natural light in while maintaining privacy." Three large tall windows face the side porch and garden. A single tall window looks out to the street, where its decorous presence evokes, but does not reveal, the complex hierarchy of spaces within.

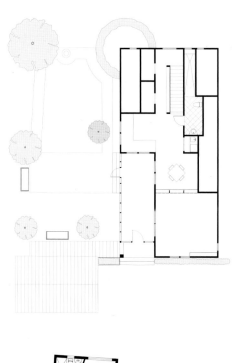

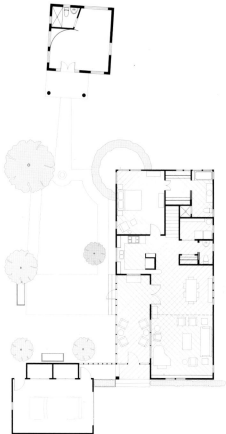

Public and Private

Collins House and Gallery
Los Angeles, California
1,400 square feet
Architect: Tighe Architecture

This remarkable building in southern California might appear to have little in common with the Rogers House in Mississippi. Their architectural languages are a continent apart. One is an adaptation of vernacular plans and forms indigenous to the American South. The other is an assertive assemblage of modernist volumes that seems tailor-made for West Hollywood.

What the two projects share, despite their aesthetic differences, are strong plans based on rigorous hierarchies. In the Collins House and Gallery, the hierarchy is all about separating public from private.

Patrick Tighe's clients are art dealers. They presented him with a considerable challenge: a single small building that would combine the public functions of an art gallery with the private functions of a house. The building he designed for them accommodates large gatherings for openings and exhibits as easily as it accommodates the daily routines of domestic life.

The clients chose the site in West Hollywood for its proximity to other art galleries. They purchased a 1,400-square-foot teardown on a four-thousand-square-foot lot. "City regulations," recalls Tighe, "required that the existing square footage and footprint be maintained and that 50 percent of the walls remain intact."

Creating a spacious gallery alone within this small, constrained footprint would have been a tall order. Combining it with a residence might have seemed impossible to an architect of lesser abilities. Tighe saw the challenge not as a difficulty to overcome but as a paradox from which to draw inspiration. The need to merge public and private under one roof inspired him to attack the problem with a single deft stroke. He bisected the building diagonally with a new load-bearing wall.

The new wall creates two distinct zones, one public and the other private. The public zone contains the long wedge-shaped gallery. The private zone contains a den, a kitchen, a bedroom, and two bathrooms. The diagonal wall is pierced to create connections between the gallery and the private rooms. This allows the gallery, in its off-hours, to double as living area and circulation. When the gallery is open, sliding partitions of opaque glass keep the private zone private.

As it turned out, Tighe never did combine public and private under a single roof. He had a better idea. He lifted the roof plane over the gallery, allowing light to enter through clerestory windows. Then he pitched it to the rear. In combination with the skewed wall, this pitched roof plane creates a powerful forced perspective, like something in a De Chirico painting. "The space tapers," he explains, "in plan and in section out to the garden courtyard beyond." A twenty-foot-long reflecting pool asserts the primacy of the gallery space by extending its floor plane, and thus its perceived space, beyond the building envelope.

Tighe chose building materials to articulate the hierarchy of public and private. On the street front, a storefront curtain wall of aluminum framing and opaque glass articulates the gallery. "The curtain wall," says Tighe, "continues above the roof plane to give the facade a more commanding presence. The form on the right is a more expressive piece clad with interlocking panels of zinc and denotes the residence." The void between public and private is a recessed transparent entrance. It has been elegantly reduced to little more than a five-foot-wide steel-framed glass panel that pivots open over a stainless-steel threshold. "It's a grand arrival," notes Tighe, "into a relatively small building."

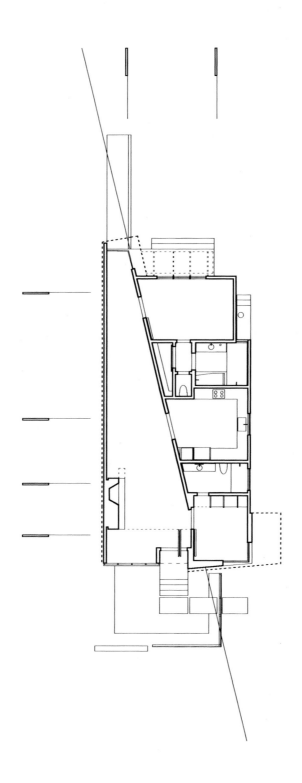

Light

No space, architecturally, is a space unless
it has natural light.

Louis Kahn

Without light, architecture is imperceptible. Sunlight, in particular, not only illuminates the exterior forms and interior spaces of our homes, it animates them. The color and mood of the sky, along with the interplay of shade and shadow, are powerful architectural elements, produced by the intensity and angle of sunlight as it shifts throughout the day. These can be used to great advantage in the design of small dwellings.

Look at virtually any photograph in this book, and you will see that light falling on forms and surfaces is what really brings architecture to life. Light brings focus to form, accentuates color, and articulates texture. When a house is said to have a soul, light has a lot to do with it. When an interior is said to have warmth, light is usually the reason.

The architect who knows how to manipulate light has a powerful tool at his disposal in the design of small dwellings. By carefully locating and orienting windows and their variants—skylights, glass walls, and glass doors— he can control how light enters an interior to illuminate its surfaces and forms. In a freestanding house, this is an easier task. All of the elevations are available for windows. In an urban row house or apartment, there are limits. Windows may exist on only one or two elevations, leaving some interior spaces dark. In these situations, light can get a boost from other architectural principles such as scale, transparency, and spatial layering. Windows can be overscaled at the perimeter layer of space to bring sunlight to the interior layers. An open plan can allow multiple spaces to benefit from the perceived light of a distant window. Walls of translucent or clear glass or plastic can be used to enclose spaces with no windows. And skylights can be used to crown vertical elements like stairs with overhead light.

In a freestanding house, where access to daylight is easier, light works in the service of hierarchy. The primary space of any dwelling should have the best orientation to daylight. Wherever possible, this means at least two, or better yet three, exposures. Multiple exposures allow daylight to enter from multiple directions. They provide natural light throughout the day. They provide an awareness of the path of the sun and the changing color of the sky. They prevent glare. And they provide cross ventilation. It's easier to achieve all of this in a small house, where the primary space can often be given three exposures, and even the secondary spaces are likely to have two.

Of course, light generally does make a small space seem larger. But it also does something more. It transforms a small space into art. Whether it's the high-contrast rake of southern light or the soft diffusion of northern light, it washes over a space and reveals not its size but its soul.

A Skylight Glows in Brooklyn

Coburn Ceccarelli Apartment
Brooklyn, New York
1,700 square feet
Architect: Coburn Architecture PC

By New York standards, the smallness of this triplex apartment is debatable. Even investment bankers have been known to lust after 1,700 square feet in Cobble Hill, one of Brooklyn's better neighborhoods. But the square footage alone doesn't tell the whole story. This light and spacious home has been carved out of a badly deteriorated brownstone only sixteen feet wide. Like most row houses, it was badly in need of light.

Architect Brendan Coburn grew up in a row house. For much of the day, even its windowed rooms received little direct light, and its inner spaces received none at all. His house was twenty feet wide, generous as row houses go, and had a decent number of windows on the front and back facades. It also had a skylight over the stair. Nonetheless, the inner spaces away from the windows were mostly dark. "I think I grew up," says Coburn, "profoundly aware of the difficulty in getting light into the inner spaces of the house."

Row houses are constrained not only by a lack of light but also by the way their stairs cramp the layout of rooms. Typically the stair is set parallel to the side wall, close to the front door. The unfortunate result is that on every floor, the width of the front room is substantially reduced. Coburn learned how to solve both problems when he was a student working for his architect parents. They designed renovations of row houses with widths as meager as fourteen feet and as grand as twenty-five feet. Coburn preferred the meager ones.

> The fourteen- and sixteen-foot houses were fascinating because their narrowness required the stair to be moved to the center of the building… With a skylight atop the stair tower, these houses were the brightest and most pleasant of the small row houses I had seen. Additionally, the stair in the middle allowed the front and back rooms to be the full width of the house. These two design moves ended up creating a lightness and elegance that was more pleasing than the larger twenty- to twenty-five-foot row houses that we also worked on.

Coburn's preference for narrow space was still with him when he and his wife, Bertina Ceccarelli, decided to buy their own small row house in Brooklyn. By now, his preference was bolstered by skill, experience, and daring. When the existing building proved too small and too fragile, Coburn had everything behind the nineteenth-century street facade demolished. In its place he designed a two-family house whose layout embodied his childhood longing for more light and his student lesson on the optimal placement of stairs.

In Coburn and Ceccarelli's triplex, the parlor floor is now a single loftlike space that accommodates living, dining, and kitchen areas. It has generous windows on both the street and garden facades. The garden windows give the house a much stronger relationship to the outdoors than is typical in city dwellings. They also provide southern light. In the winter, when the sun is low and gentle, and the light is welcome, it penetrates deep into the house. In the summer, when the sun is high and harsh, and the light needs to be controlled, it is modulated by a cantilevered cedar *brise-soleil* (louvered sun screen).

Locating the stair in the center, perpendicular to the length of the house, allows the living and dining areas and the bedrooms above to enjoy the house's full sixteen-foot width. A rather elaborate skylight illuminates the open stair from above. It also opens to provide ventilation.

Most ingenious of all are the oversized stair landings, which double as home offices. Their floors are made of glass. Because of them, what would normally be the darkest parts of the house are now bathed in a soft glow of light.

Santa Monica Lighthouse

745 Navy Street
Santa Monica, California
700 square feet
Architect: Joel Blank and Susie Tsay Tashiro Architects

This tiny remodeled house suffered all the usual constraints of a small house on a long, narrow urban lot: a tight footprint that could not, by local code, be enlarged; narrow and hard to use outdoor spaces along the sides; and difficulty getting light to the middle. It was also constrained by a small budget.

Architects Joel Blank and Susie Tsay Tashiro resolved these problems with great economy of means. They devised a limited but inventive vocabulary of design elements that endowed this little house with openness, transparency between indoors and out, and the perception of greater volume. Most significantly, they enhanced the perception of light.

The architects literally started at the ground and worked their way up. They replaced the existing raised floor with a new concrete slab on grade. This made the interior and exterior floor levels the same, thereby helping to erase the boundary between indoors and out. They also removed the existing ceiling to expose the structural rhythm of the rafters and create additional height.

The problem of the narrow and awkward side yards required a two-pronged attack. First came new fencing at the lot line. This fencing, made of simple horizontal wood slats, had to be good-looking enough for both indoors and out, because it effectively became the exterior wall of the house as seen from inside.

Ordinarily, the side elevations of an urban house on a narrow lot would have, at best, poky little clerestory windows and the limited light they imply. But the privacy and controlled views created by the new fencing allowed the use of large floor-to-ceiling windows. These transformed the side yards into layers of space that expand the house visually into the side yards. They also allowed the interior to be flooded with light from the sides.

A second lighting element is the skylight. Five of them sit atop the gable roof toward the front of the house, giving it a sculptural presence. They face north, as skylights should, and provide a soft, ambient light. They are motorized, so in warm weather, they open to cool the spaces below.

The third design element addressing the issue of light is the translucent wall separating kitchen and living room from den and bathroom. It is made of corrugated polycarbonate panels, which conceal fluorescent light strips. "This provides its container," says Joel Blank, "with scale, contrast, and an enriched spatial composition." On a more basic level, it houses all the plumbing for the kitchen and bath. It also serves as an ambient light source for all rooms except the bedroom. The warm glow of the translucent wall takes a boundary between spaces and transforms it into a luminous suggestion of space beyond.

Seven hundred square feet, artfully layered and lit, can be a lot of house.

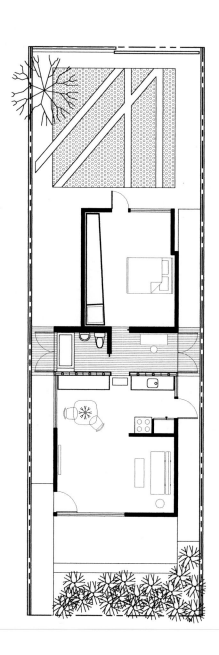

Multifunctionalism

Beauty depends on fitness, and the
practical requirements of life are the
ultimate test of fitness.

Edith Wharton

Every space in a small dwelling has to earn its square footage by playing several roles. The notion of multiple enclosed rooms is considered traditional but is actually rather new. Until the Renaissance, the norm was a single large room used for eating, sleeping, cooking, bathing, and socializing. Privacy, when required, was provided by portable means such as screens and hangings. Furniture was simply rearranged to accommodate different activities.

   The concept of an individual room for each individual function dates back only to the nineteenth century. One of the great luxuries of the Victorian house was that it had separate rooms for everything: parlors, sitting rooms, drawing rooms, studies, libraries, offices, boudoirs, bedrooms, dressing rooms, water closets, bathrooms, kitchens, pantries, sculleries, and more. It took a lot of money and a lot of servants to keep all that going.

   Most of these redundant rooms, and the society that supported them, have not survived. What has endured is the notion that each function in our lives should have an individual enclosed space. This is surprising, because the idea of the open plan has been kicking around for over a hundred years. It has caught on in urban lofts and some architect-designed houses. And you do hear occasionally about Park Avenue matrons who are gutting their eight-room prewar apartments to get "a loftlike feeling." But most new dwellings bigger than a studio apartment are still laid out with multiple fully enclosed rooms. The problem is that all those rooms add up to more square footage, which adds up to more money. And yet they achieve little if any spatial distinction. The open plan goes hand in hand with multifunctionalism. It offers numerous ways to get maximum function out of minimum space. It is full of practical possibilities and is hardly revolutionary. It's time we reconsider it.

The loss of separate rooms required by multifunctionalism is not a hardship. It is instead a liberation from outmoded conventions. It is an opportunity to do more with less.

Beyond Functional

Harrison House
Nashville, Tennessee
2,100 square feet
Architect: Price Harrison Architects + Associates PLLC

The house that Price Harrison designed for himself and his wife, Dr. Stacy Davis Harrison, is exemplary in so many ways that to choose it as an example of multi-functionalism seems arbitrary. It could just as easily illustrate most of the other architectural principles essential to good small dwellings. Its plan of parallel zones exemplifies proportion, spatial layering, and modularity. Its clear separation of public and private spaces is an object lesson in hierarchy and procession. And its deft handling of windows combines the lessons of both scale and light. But if ever there was a space that combined multiple functions with extraordinary elegance, it is the combined living, dining, and kitchen area of this house.

Advising architects and their clients to strive for multifunctionalism is a bit like telling children to eat their vegetables. It may be good for them, but it doesn't sound very appealing. It can conjure up images of tenement apartments with bathtubs in the kitchen and of houses where dinner is eaten in full view of all the dirty pots and pans. It can make us long for a house with a proper kitchen, living room, and dining room. But the multipurpose public space of Price Harrison's house is so refined and so luxe that it makes all such preconceptions and longings disappear.

Harrison organized his house in a manner that recalls the rigorous asymmetrical plans of Mies van der Rohe. It consists of two solid rectangular volumes that slide past each other. The longer volume houses the garage and the private spaces. The shorter volume contains the public space. The transparent void between the two volumes links them and serves as the entry.

Harrison underscored the importance of the public volume with two deft moves. First, he gave it grand proportions. It is ten feet high by twenty feet wide by forty feet long. These are the proportions of a noble and important room. Second, he provided it with windows on all four sides, an ideal condition that is much more difficult to achieve in a large house.

A room with these qualities of light and proportion would ennoble any function that takes place within it. In Harrison's house, it ennobles three functions: living, dining, and kitchen. And yet the room accommodates these functions in a livable, even casual, manner. "All of the spaces are used everyday," says Harrison. "There are no formal spaces."

The room assigns each function a specific location. The long double-galley kitchen is centered on the south wall close to the entry. It acts as an anchor, a solid between entry on one side and windows on the other. One half of the kitchen is concealed by tall cabinetry. The other half is open to the living area, which allows the Harrisons to prepare dinner while talking to guests. Living and dining each occupy half of the remaining long, narrow rectangle parallel to the kitchen. Overscaled windows, in asymmetrical compositions of glass and mahogany, wrap the corners and keep these areas from feeling like furniture groupings floating in a void. The windows provide transparent anchors for living and dining in counterpoint to the solid anchor of the kitchen.

Furniture and finishes play an important role in this room. You cannot combine multiple functions in a single space with any aesthetic success unless all the functions share a palette of harmonious colors and materials. Fortunately, Harrison had some expert help from his mother, Marilyn McMackin, a gifted interior designer who converted to her son's brand of ascetic modernism several years ago when he designed her house. Together they developed a limited but refined palette, consisting mostly of white with accents of chocolate brown, and applied it as artfully to cabinets as they did to upholstery. Their collaborative brand of high-style minimalism makes multifunctionalism seem like the height of luxury.

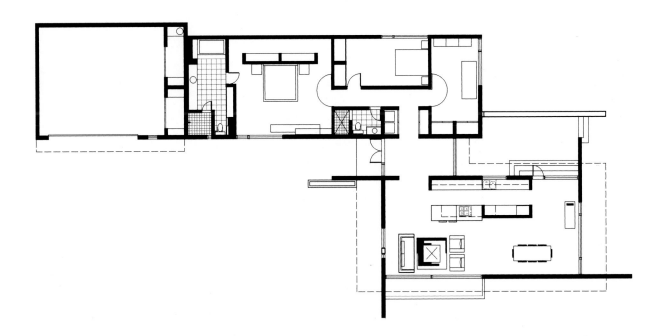

Simplicity

I adore simple pleasures. They are the last refuge of the complex.

Oscar Wilde

The virtue of simplicity is desirable anywhere, but in a small house or apartment, it is mandatory. Nothing kills the exterior beauty of a small house like needlessly complex massing, too many different door and window types, and too many different materials and details. And nothing kills a small interior space like *horror vacui*. Space is a great luxury, especially in a small home. It shouldn't be squandered on too many small rooms, too much furniture, too many knickknacks, or too many discordant details and finishes. "Simplicity," wrote Edith Wharton, "is the supreme excellence."

Fashion legend Coco Chanel once advised stylish women to remove one thing—a piece of jewelry, a scarf or other accessory—before they went out. The point was that a woman is more likely to be chic wearing less rather than more. Style is more likely to thrive in simplicity than in complexity. Fashionable women have been following this advice for almost a century. And yet many women—and men too, for that matter—cannot extend this principle to their homes. Women who wouldn't be caught dead wearing fringe and flounces will gladly attach them to their sofas and draperies. Men who pride themselves on being meticulously organized at work live with endless piles of clutter at home. And clients who pride themselves on clear thinking allow themselves to be talked into muddled complexities in the design of their homes.

In a large home where space permits, fringe and flounces and piles of clutter are a matter of taste and might even have a certain charm. But in a small home, they are deadly. They suck up all the space just as a too talkative guest sucks up all the air. A small home with simple architectural details and finishes, simple furnishings, and simple accessories can be smart and stylish. The same home filled with too much stuff can be squalid and stifling.

A small house or apartment is no place to be fussy. There is simply no room for it. A clear, straightforward plan with a single strong architectural idea will make the most of limited space. Architectural details should be streamlined lest they distract from the space rather than reinforce it. Materials and details should be chosen with an eye to harmony in a limited color palette. And furniture must be carefully laid out and chosen first and foremost for scale. If the furniture can also reinforce the underlying architectural idea, all the better.

Simplicity, to paraphrase Edith Wharton, is at home anywhere, but it doesn't just happen. It takes vision and the discipline to pursue it. It takes an ability to establish simple goals and achieve them with simple means. It takes a commitment to creating the sort of harmony that can come only from less rather than more.

The Poetics
of Simplicity

Finney House
Philadelphia, Pennsylvania
1,450 square feet
Architect: M. Finney Design

If we could measure our fortune by the quality of our housing, Martha Finney's initials would have a second meaning: Most Fortunate. Within the city limits of Philadelphia, she has created an idyll of rural simplicity. The site is an old farm at the crest of a hill high above the Schuylkill River. The house was the abandoned shell of an old stone farmhouse dating back to 1809. The program called for the renovation of the house and the replacement of an existing addition. The client was Martha Finney herself, a single-minded young woman with a few simple goals and limited means to achieve them.

The gabled form of an old stone house can be very seductive in its simplicity. It can also be very dark. These houses were built primarily for shelter. Their thick masonry walls kept out heat in the summer and cold in the winter. Openings in the stone walls let those elements in. And glass was expensive. So windows tended to be small and few, and interiors were often gloomy. In Finney's house the division of the interior into small rooms exacerbated the darkness.

"The idea," says Finney, "was to open the house to the outside, to give the interior a feeling of spaciousness and to orchestrate the movement through the house so that no matter where you stood in a room you were able to see through a second space and out to the woods."

Finney's goals were transparency and spatial layering, and the means by which she achieved them couldn't have been simpler. She started by reducing the number of rooms. On the first floor, by removing just one wall, she banished two cramped little rooms and created one generous living room. "The second floor," she explains, "had been two rooms and a corridor. I removed all but a section of wall, leaving the second floor with the feel of one room but the privacy of two."

Another of Finney's goals was scale. She wanted the scale of the new to be consistent with the scale of the old. The new addition, she explains, "sits on the footprint of the old. From the outside it was to look as if it had alit for just a moment, to say hello and move on, leaving the solid stone structure intact." The need for an appropriate scale for new elements in relation to old also influenced her moves indoors. Again, simplicity guided her toward efficient solutions. The kitchen, for example, is separated from the dining area by little more than two cabinets. These, says Finney, "define an opening but do not limit the free flow of space and light."

Simplicity also determined Finney's choices of materials: painted wood walls and trim, plaster ceilings, and painted pine floors. A single utilitarian light fixture is repeated throughout. But the simplicity of these choices goes beyond utility and into the realm of poetry. "I wanted to use materials that might have been around in 1809," explains Finney, "and use them to animate the old, usher in the new. I like to think of architecture as kinesthetic and to use materials and structure to create a sense of hazy familiarity."

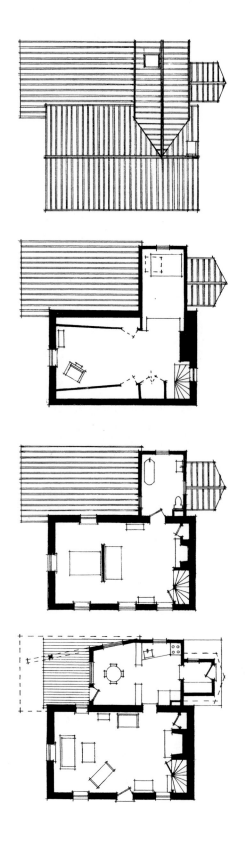

Economy

If three rooms meet the requirements of
your family, or if they are all you can afford,
why build more?

The Architects' Small House Service Bureau

If excess is the enemy of simplicity, then economy is its handmaid. Economy makes simplicity possible. Without it, simplicity could not exist. But economy is not only a means to simplicity. It is a worthy goal in its own right. The fundamental rule of economy is that there is no direct ratio between quantity and quality. More does not mean better.

Economy comes in several guises. Architects refer to "economy of means." This refers not to construction cost, but to the ability to create a compelling design with just a few deft moves. The designs of Mies van der Rohe, for example, are often said to have great economy of means because their plans are straightforward, their materials are few, and their details are simple. Full disclosure: economy of means doesn't always come cheap. Mies's buildings, no matter how simple, were always expensive.

Another kind of economy has everything to do with cost. This kind of economy comes from the deliberate selection of things that cost less. Two thousand square feet of house will cost less than three thousand. A galvanized aluminum roof will cost less than slate. Stock size doors and windows will cost less than custom. Choices like these can generate significant savings with no significant loss of quality. What costs less can often be worth more.

A third kind of economy is about attitude. It's about getting a little thrill out of doing more with less. It requires that architect and client get excited about the possibilities for elegance and inventiveness in a compact floor plan. And it requires a bit of self-examination. Are fifty pairs of shoes really necessary if the closets for them will overwhelm a small space? If large dinner parties aren't that much fun, why bemoan the lack of a formal dining room? Are industrial-strength appliances really necessary for a modest amount of cooking? You can't have economy without making choices.

To be economical means to do only what is essential. Anything more will only preclude the simplicity that is fundamental to living well. Let go of the nonessential. You are unlikely to miss it, and the freedom will be exhilarating. Mies was right. Less really is more.

A Wedge
in the Woods

Bartholomew House
The Catskills, New York
1,600 square feet
Architect: Ryall Porter Architects

Ryall Porter Architects designed this modest weekend getaway for two New Yorkers, one a poet and bartender and the other a professor. Their program required two bedrooms and two baths with an open kitchen/living/dining area, and a study/loft to serve as a third bedroom. Their site was a long narrow lot next to a small lake. Their budget was tight.

The architects' design for this rural retreat was influenced by urban sources, such as simple industrial buildings and open loft spaces. Their *parti,* which resolved program, site, and budget, is an elegant example of economy in all three of its meanings: economy of means, economy of cost, and economy of attitude.

Economy of means is embodied in the form of the house: a simple wedge. The wedge resulted from a rectangular plan and a shed roof with its slope running the length of the rectangle. The wedge shape accommodated the clients' program naturally. "The bedrooms and bathrooms," explains project architect Ted Sheridan, "were stacked under the high side of the wedge, allowing the kitchen/dining/living area to have a one-

and-a-half-story height. Emphasis was placed on the lake view, but high windows were positioned on other facades to maximize and balance natural light levels."

In addition to the wedge is a screen porch on the lakeside elevation. This porch is not just added on to the volume of the house. Instead, it is integrated into the house via a partial recess. The porch provides a secondary scale and strengthens the visual relationship between the woods, the house, and the lake. These are among the many skillful moves that give this house a sophistication well beyond its budget.

Economy of cost made economy of means possible. In an area where custom-home costs can typically exceed $200 per square foot, the general contractor brought this house in for $115 per square foot. Sheridan's approach to cost started with organizing the house on a four-foot module, the standard for many building materials, to minimize waste. And the entire house, with the exception of the exterior metal siding, was specified from the Home Depot's supply catalog. Among the more effective cheap products used is the birch veneer plywood ceiling. It turned the ceiling plane into a powerful architectural element, but because it required no taping, spackling, or painting, it was only marginally more expensive than Sheetrock.

Economy of attitude? Well, the photos speak for themselves. "Primary forms," wrote Le Corbusier, "are beautiful forms because they can be clearly appreciated." Ryall Porter Architects saw a tight budget not as a limitation but as an opportunity, which he used to create a primary form of great comfort and clarity.

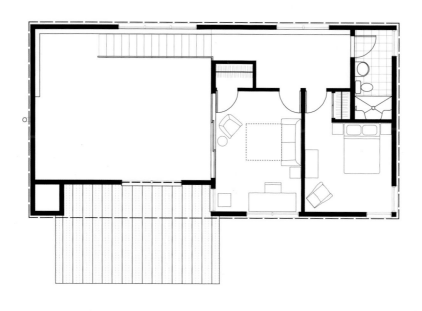

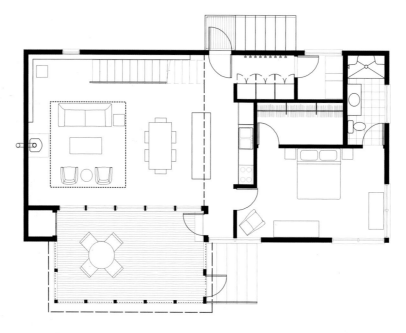

A Wedge
in the Woods

Bartholomew House
The Catskills, New York
1,600 square feet
Architect: Ryall Porter Architects

Ryall Porter Architects designed this modest weekend getaway for two New Yorkers, one a poet and bartender and the other a professor. Their program required two bedrooms and two baths with an open kitchen/living/dining area, and a study/loft to serve as a third bedroom. Their site was a long narrow lot next to a small lake. Their budget was tight.

The architects' design for this rural retreat was influenced by urban sources, such as simple industrial buildings and open loft spaces. Their *parti,* which resolved program, site, and budget, is an elegant example of economy in all three of its meanings: economy of means, economy of cost, and economy of attitude.

Economy of means is embodied in the form of the house: a simple wedge. The wedge resulted from a rectangular plan and a shed roof with its slope running the length of the rectangle. The wedge shape accommodated the clients' program naturally. "The bedrooms and bathrooms," explains project architect Ted Sheridan, "were stacked under the high side of the wedge, allowing the kitchen/dining/living area to have a one-

and-a-half-story height. Emphasis was placed on the lake view, but high windows were positioned on other facades to maximize and balance natural light levels."

In addition to the wedge is a screen porch on the lakeside elevation. This porch is not just added on to the volume of the house. Instead, it is integrated into the house via a partial recess. The porch provides a secondary scale and strengthens the visual relationship between the woods, the house, and the lake. These are among the many skillful moves that give this house a sophistication well beyond its budget.

Economy of cost made economy of means possible. In an area where custom-home costs can typically exceed $200 per square foot, the general contractor brought this house in for $115 per square foot. Sheridan's approach to cost started with organizing the house on a four-foot module, the standard for many building materials, to minimize waste. And the entire house, with the exception of the exterior metal siding, was specified from the Home Depot's supply catalog. Among the more effective cheap products used is the birch veneer plywood ceiling. It turned the ceiling plane into a powerful architectural element, but because it required no taping, spackling, or painting, it was only marginally more expensive than Sheetrock.

Economy of attitude? Well, the photos speak for themselves. "Primary forms," wrote Le Corbusier, "are beautiful forms because they can be clearly appreciated." Ryall Porter Architects saw a tight budget not as a limitation but as an opportunity, which he used to create a primary form of great comfort and clarity.

Modesty

Modesty is the citadel of beauty.

Demades, ancient Athenian orator

The tenth principle is modesty. Modesty requires us to arrange our homes to suit the real needs of our private lives with no thought of public display. It requires us to embrace the appropriate and the suitable. It requires us to eschew the showy and the unnecessary. And it requires us to reject the notion that our homes must be public indicators of status and ambition. They should instead be private refuges of relaxed suitability.

A small home should be highly desirable on its own terms. It should not attempt to look like anything more than what it is. A small apartment, its rooms simply planned and minimally furnished with a few good pieces of suitable scale, can be comfortable and stylish. The same small apartment, its walls slathered with mirrors to make it look twice its size and its rooms bursting with overscaled furniture and must-have appliances, is likely to be grotesque. A small cottage with simple massing, of modest vernacular scale and style, can be charming. A house of similar size, tarted up with a cacophony of architectural elements for the sake of "curb appeal," is likely to be hideous. A cottage is not a mansion, nor should it be.

Modesty can challenge architects for two reasons. First, it is antithetical to the cult of artistic self-expression, which confuses art and creativity with self-conscious originality. But modesty does not preclude art or creativity. Indeed, it encourages them. It precludes only vanity, hubris, and self-indulgence. In architecture, as in life, these are characteristics to be shunned. In small dwellings, these are characteristics for which there is simply no room.

Second, small dwellings are often the work of the profession's youngest members, who have energy, ambition, and plenty of ideas. Unfortunately, they sometimes see the design of that one little house or apartment as an opportunity to explore all of those ideas at once. And so the small dwelling becomes a hodgepodge of multiple architectural ideas. For a small house or apartment, one good idea is all it takes.

Clients, too, can have modesty issues. They, too, may feel the urge for artistic self-expression. It's bad enough when the architect succumbs to this malady, but if both client and architect are looking for artistic self-expression in a single small home, the result can be anything but artistic. Also problematic is the urge to impress. We all, on some level, need to affirm our self-worth by impressing family, friends, neighbors, and others. But a beautifully designed small home can be very impressive on its own terms. There's no need to gussy it up, pack it with too much stuff, or apologize for its size. Modesty means never having to say you're sorry.

In a small home there is no room for pretension and the insecurity that feeds it. Unhappiness is both cause and effect of these afflictions. Modesty is both prevention and cure.

Rice Welch Apartment
New York, New York
475 square feet
Architects: Ward Welch and Paul Rice

The apartment that Welch and Rice bought in the West Village defined modesty. It was that most humble of urban housing types, the cold-water flat in a walk-up tenement building. This apartment type is also known as a railroad flat because of the way its long narrow rooms are strung out from front to back without halls for circulation. It had four rooms, two without windows, with a toilet and sink at one end and a tub in the kitchen at the other.

The overall length of the apartment is fifty feet. The width is eleven feet at the ends and eight feet in the middle. Windows exist only at the ends. The shape is essentially a dumbbell: two rooms connected by a narrow rectangular bar. In their beach house, Welch and Rice considered many different plan schemes. In the apartment, however, the options were very limited. "The apartment," said Welch, "seemed to design itself from the circumstances its gutted shell presented." These circumstances dictated living area and bedroom at the windowed ends and kitchen, bath and dressing area in the narrow middle. The plan is simple and largely predetermined, with no room for immodest architectural gestures.

The clear logic of this scheme did not make it easy to achieve. Moving the kitchen and bath from the ends to the middle required extensive plumbing relocations. It also deprived both spaces of windows. And the undulation of the apartment's south wall meant that some spaces were destined to have irregular shapes.

The architects made virtues of these vices. Some of the plumbing runs became an occasion to level the floors that contain them. The build-out needed to carry the wall-hung toilet provided space above for much needed storage. The kitchen is completely open to the living area's east-facing windows and so gets an abundance of borrowed light. The windowless bathroom borrows light from the adjacent bedroom through a floor-to-ceiling frosted glass panel. And the undulating wall provides a recess for the toilet and a closet for the laundry. "The inconsistencies of the shell define all aspects of the space," explains Welch. "No space is wasted, none taken for granted."

The kitchen in particular is a good example of how modesty, in tandem with common sense, drives the plan of this apartment. The eight-foot width of the available space meant that the kitchen would have to double as circulation. An architect or client trying to impose immodest ambitions on this little apartment and make it grander than it was meant to be would have found this troubling. He might have tortured the plan until it provided some artificial separation between the two functions. Instead, the architects laid out the kitchen as a straightforward double galley with four feet of circulation and simple painted cabinetry. Is it an efficient kitchen or a generous hall lined with cabinetry? The answer is both.

To attain a level of richness and simplicity, the architects chose a muted color palette of dark woods paired with warm whites and beiges. The effect is rather like a small suite in a smart boutique hotel, a suitably urbane style for a small urban space. "As with the Amagansett house," explains Rice, "we wanted an architectural aesthetic of subtlety and simple elegance, which would maximize space without magnifying the lack of it, but also respect the diminutive character of both places and let it guide the design process." He goes on to summarize the essence of modesty. "We sought to determine what was essential, and anything not needed was not done."

220

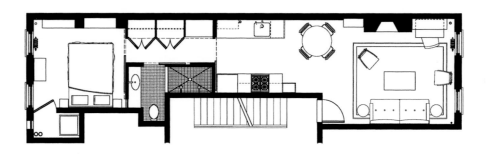

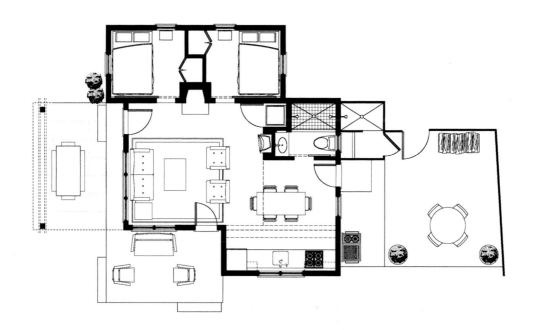

Small at the Beach and Small in the Village: Two Elegant Essays in Modesty

This very small eastern Long Island beach house and even smaller Greenwich Village apartment exemplify a refined and elegant brand of modesty in a complementary pair of small dwellings that two New York architects call home.

Rice Welch House
Amagansett, New York
520 square feet
Architects: Ward Welch and Paul Rice

Ward Welch and Paul Rice view the simplicity and smallness of their urban and rural homes as a product of their financial status. "But to a greater degree," says Welch, these qualities "are a much sought-after prize." There are two reasons for this. First, because their limited budgets are concentrated in small areas, they allow the two architects to enjoy a high level of quality in their homes. Second, these small dwellings fulfill deeply rooted childhood desires for well-defined spaces.

Their beach house had begun its life as a three-hundred-square-foot fishing shack. Over time its porch had been enclosed and two small wings added. When Welch and Rice bought it, its total size was 520 square feet, all on one level. Local zoning regulations precluded enlarging the footprint of the house. Undeterred, the owners were confident that the existing space could be reconfigured to accommodate their own basic needs plus an occasional overnight guest and dinner party, "without the final product being about smallness," recalls Rice.

The modesty of the program suited the modesty of the cottage. It consisted of two bedrooms, a bathroom, laundry, storage, kitchen, dining and living areas, and outdoor space. The architects examined many schemes in an effort to maximize living space within the cottage's limited confines. Despite the modest program, the chosen scheme established a clear spatial hierarchy. The living area was given pride of place—and the highest ceiling—by placing it under the main gable of the roof. All other spaces were arranged around the living area in a pecking order based on light and quiet.

The house strikes a skillful balance between discrete rooms and open space. "The size of the house," explains Welch, "made it all the more necessary to make the rooms within feel special. Though the spaces are clearly defined, the plan's openness makes it feel like one big room with alcoves." Low ceilings were removed, exposing additional height up to the rafters. Devices used to maximize floor space include built-in cabinets and sliding door panels. The fireplace is detailed as minimally as possible, and the tiny twin bedrooms flanking it are treated as ship's berths. These features were born of necessity, but they exert a powerful charm.

The exterior of the house maintains the modesty of the interior. Cedar decks and an ivy-covered trellis embellish the simple massing and extend the limited interior space outdoors. The architectural language never strays far from the local vernacular. Cedar shingles accented by crisp white windows, doors, and trim make this an iconic eastern Long Island beach cottage.

Welch and Rice's ambitions for this cottage were well suited to its modest character and scale, and they achieved them through suitably modest means. The result is a house of great charm and serenity where nothing seems forced and everything seems right. As for their initial concern that the final product not be "about smallness," they needn't have worried. Modesty, coupled with talent, skill, and an unerring eye, has taken this former shack far beyond smallness.

Four
How Big Small Can Be: The Case for Small Dwellings

A house of...extreme simplicity... makes for the ideal home, where there will be, as Henry James says, "things blissfully few and adorably good."

Eloise Roorbach, architecture critic, on the work of Irving Gill

"Living well," wrote English poet George Herbert "is the best revenge." Revenge may be too harsh a reaction to the cult of bigness, but at the very least we can offer defiance. We can do so by living well in small, skillfully designed dwellings of extreme simplicity and suitability. Such dwellings can actually deliver the good life that larger and more pretentious homes can only promise.

More modest housing will bring us several benefits, both quantitative and qualitative. The initial cost of construction will be lower, as will the cost of maintenance, especially fuel bills. Our lives will be calmer and more serene because the stress of shelling out timely payments for mortgage, taxes, insurance, and utilities will be reduced. And society will reap environmental benefits thanks to reduced consumption of limited resources.

Smaller dwellings will increase opportunities for better design because small spaces can intensify the architectural experience. More comfort and elegance will be possible, as evidenced by the dwellings in this book, because architectural creativity and construction budgets won't be squandered on excessive square footage and fetishized "luxury" materials. Instead, they will be spent where they count: on the skillful manipulation of space, artfully designed and simply crafted.

Architectural styles may come and go, but the value of architecturally distinguished small dwellings transcends style. No one architectural idiom is more likely than another to produce good small dwellings. At one end of the historical spectrum are the romantic Gothic Revival cottages of Andrew Jackson Downing. At the other end is the high modern International Style seen in the Farnsworth House by Mies van der Rohe. Both are superb. Both are seminal. Both provide foundations on which to build work of equivalent or better quality today.

The small dwellings featured in this book are evidence that today's architects are building on those diverse foundations. Their work adheres to no one style. It runs the gamut from the charming and easygoing farmhouse vernacular of the Finney House to the rigorous high-style modernity of the Harrison House. The range of approaches and aesthetics is broad enough to accommodate the taut, luxe urbanity of my own miniature penthouse as easily as it does the casual prefabrication of Jack Frederick's tiny apartment in a barn. All of these dwellings are stylish, but none of them is fundamentally about style. What they are about is a set of basic architectural principles activated by art, by craft, and by a belief that small dwellings are not only good. They are better.

The art of living well is not necessarily a simple thing. Yet it seems to thrive in a simple setting. If it is true that a rich man is as likely to enter the kingdom of heaven as is a camel to pass through the eye of a needle, then there are two corollary truths. First, a gracious and comfortable life is more likely to flourish in a small and simple home than in a large and elaborate one. This is because small dwellings are more likely to have the straightforward ease and authenticity that make a gracious home.

The second corollary truth is this: Human beings are more likely to be happy in spaces of human scale. Modest households of good design and simple elegance can bring great pleasure and satisfaction. The scale of our homes should derive from the real needs of our daily lives, not from vanity, insecurity, or a need for public display. Home should be the setting for life, not the measure of it.

Afterword:
"Nuns Fret Not at Their Convent's Narrow Room"

Nuns fret not at their convent's narrow room
And hermits are contented with their cells;
And students with their pensive citadels;
Maids at the wheel, the weaver at his loom,
Sit blithe and happy; bees that soar for bloom,
High as the highest Peak of Furness-fells,
Will murmur by the hour in foxglove bells:
In truth the prison, into which we doom
Ourselves, no prison is: and hence for me,
In sundry moods, 'twas pastime to be bound
Within the Sonnet's scanty plot of ground;
Pleased if some Souls (for such there needs must be)
Who have felt the weight of too much liberty,
Should find brief solace there, as I have found.

William Wordsworth

Select Bibliography

Alpern, Andrew. *Apartments for the Affluent: A Historical Survey Of Buildings in New York.* New York: McGraw-Hill, 1975.

Bachelard, Gaston. *The Poetics of Space: The Classic Look at How We Experience Intimate Places.* Boston: Beacon Press, 1994.

Benson, E. F. *Mapp and Lucia.* Wakefield, R.I.: Moyer Bell, 2000.

Blaser, Werner. *Mies Van Der Rohe: Furniture and Interiors.* Hauppauge, N.Y.: Barron's Educational Series, 1982.

Ching, Francis D. K. *Architecture: Form, Space and Order.* New York: John Wiley & Sons, 1995.

Clements, Jonathan. "Getting Going," *Wall Street Journal,* 19 November 2003.

Le Corbusier. *Towards a New Architecture.* Mineola, N.Y.: Dover Publications, 1985.

Cortissoz, Royal. *Domestic Architecture of H. T. Lindeberg.* New York: Acanthus Press, 1996.

Cromley, Elizabeth Collins. *Alone Together: A History of New York's Early Apartments.* Ithaca, N.Y.: Cornell University Press, 1990.

Durant, Stuart. *CFA Voysey.* London: Academy, 1992.

Goldberger, Paul. *The City Observed, New York.* New York: Random House, 1979.

Halsted, Byron D., ed. *Barns, Sheds and Outbuildings.* Brattleboro, Vt.: Stephen Greene Press, 1977.

Hawes, Elizabeth. *New York, New York: How the Apartment HouseTransformed the Life of the City, 1869–1930.* New York: Henry Holt & Company, 1994.

Hines, Thomas S. *Irving Gill and the Architecture of Reform: A Study in Modernist Architectural Culture.* New York: The Monacelli Press, 2000.

Hitchcock, Henry-Russell. *In the Nature of Materials, 1887–1941: The Buildings of Frank Lloyd Wright.* New York: Da Capo Press, 1973.

Jones, Robert T., ed. *Authentic Small Houses of the Twenties.* Mineola, N.Y.: Dover Publications, 1987.

McCoy, Esther. *Case Study Houses, 1945–1962.* Los Angeles: Hennessey & Ingalls, 1977.

Roth, Leland M. *A Concise History of American Architecture.* New York: Harper & Row, 1979.

Ruttenbaum, Steven. *Mansions in the Clouds: The Skyscraper Palazzi of Emery Roth.* New York: Balsam Press, 1986.

Safran, Yehuda E. *Mies Van Der Rohe.* Barcelona: GG, 2001.

Schezen, Roberto, Kenneth Frampton, and Joe Rosa. *Adolf Loos, Architecture 1903–1932.* New York: The Monacelli Press, 1996.

Scully, Vincent. *The Shingle Style and the Stick Style: Architectural Theory Design from Downing to the Origins of Wright.* New Haven, Conn.: Yale University Press, 1976.

Sergeant, John. *Frank Lloyd Wright's Usonian Houses: The Case for Organic Arcitecture.* New York: Whitney Library of Design, 1976.

Smith, Mary Ann. *Gustav Stickley, The Craftsman.* Syracuse, N.Y.: Syracuse University Press, 1983.

Stern, Robert A. M., et al. *New York 1930: Architecture and Urbanism between the Two World Wars.* New York: Rizzoli, 1987.

Tompkins, Calvin. *Living Well Is the Best Revenge.* New York: Viking, 1971.

Tournikiotis, Panayotis. *Loos.* New York: Princeton Architectural Press, 1994.

Vaill, Amanda. *Everybody Was So Young: Gerald and Sara Murphy, a Lost Generation Love Story.* Boston: Houghton-Mifflin, 1998.

Van Duzer, Leslie, and Kent Kleinman. *Villa Müller: A Work of Adfolf Loos.* New York: Princeton Architectural Press, 1994.

Weiss, Ellen. *City in the Woods: The Life and Design of an American Camp Meeting on Martha's Vineyard.* New York: Oxford University Press, 1987.

Wharton, Edith. *Italian Villas and Their Gardens.* New York: Century, 1910.

Wharton, Edith, and Ogden Codman, Jr. *The Decoration of Houses.* New York: Charles Scribner's Sons, 1897.

Thanks to my friend Jim Stewart, who first suggested
this book. To my agent, Amanda Urban, for believing in
this project even before I did. To Suzanne Stephens for
her invaluable advice and enthusiasm. To Cathy Tighe for
her beautiful photos and to her husband, Keith McPeters,
for putting up with a lot. To Kate Davis Caldwell for
keeping Cathy and me organized and to Sara Evans for
her on-site photo assistance. To Larry Tighe, Stephen
Brockman, and Julianna Morais for putting us in touch
with so many terrific architects. To Mariana Marron and
Brian Geller for helping with the original proposal and
for picking up the slack at the office while I wrote. To
Andrea Monfried, Elizabeth Kugler, and Evan Schoninger
at the Monacelli Press for being kind and patient with
a first-time author. To my aunt, M. T. Gauer, and to Blake
Auchincloss, Miro Balac, Julie Lawton, and Diane Wachs
for their encouragement. To Anne Bennett Brandenburger,
who always knew how to do more with less. To Mary
Mitchell, whose tiny apartment began my architectural
career. To Debbie and Jud Sommer and to David Wine,
for believing in me. Their houses may be a bit too big
for this book, but they're small-house people at heart.
To Donna Warner, Linda O'Keeffe, and Dan Golden at
Metropolitan Home magazine for their abiding enthusiasm
and generosity over many years. And to Joel Goldsmith
for everything.

Acknowledgments

James Gauer holds a Master of Architecture degree from Columbia University. He practices architecture at Gauer & Marron Studio in Victoria, British Columbia, and in New York City, where small spaces are inevitable.

His work includes both residential and commercial projects, which regularly appear in such publications as *Architectural Record, Canadian Interiors, Grund Genug* (Germany), *Home, House Beautiful, House & Garden, Ideat* (France), *Interior Design, Metropolitan Home,* the *New York Times,* and *Lofts.*

Some of his best projects have been small dwellings.

Catherine Tighe is based in Lambertville, New Jersey, but photographs architecture around the world. Her work has led her from utopian farmhouses in Pennsylvania to modern office buildings in Bombay.

Her photos appear frequently in such magazines as *Architectural Record, Casa Abitare, Domus, Dwell, Interior Design,* and *Metropolitan Home.*

Coburn Ceccarelli Apartment

745 Navy Street

Bartholomew House

Rice Welch House